Treasury of Supplications

Du'as of the Prophets

Islamic Supplications in Crisis and Distress

Salah Moujahed

CONTENTS

PREFACE

"This was our argument We gave Abraham against his people. We elevate in rank whoever We please. Surely Your Lord is All-Wise, All-Knowing. And We blessed him with Isaac and Jacob, We guided them all as We previously guided Noah and those among his progeny: David and Solomon and Job and Joseph and Moses and Aaron. This is how We reward the good-doers. Likewise, Zachariah and John and Jesus and Elias, who were all of the righteous. (We also guided) Ishmael, Elisha, Jonah, and Lot, favoring each over other people (of their time)."

[Surah Al-Ana'ām 6:83-86]

Many messengers have been sent by God to us humans.

"And for every community there is a messenger."

[Surah Yunus 10:47]

This book contains selected Du'ās (supplications) of special and exemplary people, the Messengers and Prophets of Allah (SWT). Some of their supplications have been passed to us from Holy Qur'ān. We know that all the Messengers were carefully chosen by Allah (SWT) and that they were of special wisdom so that they can serve as role models for us. The Qur'ān tells us their stories and shows us how they prayed to Allah (SWT), especially when they were in situations of great hardship and crises. In this way, we too can use their prayers so that Allah (SWT), hears and helps us.

The first part of this document is dedicated to the Du'ās of the prophets and messengers of Allah, from Ādam to 'Īsā' (Peace be upon them). All of these Prayers are from the Holy Qur'ān. In the second part of this document, you will find valuable supplications of Prophet Muḥammad (ﷺ), the last prophet and messenger of Allah (SWT). His life was marked by immense difficulties and crises; be it a two-year famine he had to endure or the loss of many loved ones. With the help of Allah (SWT), and his supplications, he managed to overcome all his problems, which makes him a special role model for Muslims. Many of his Du'ās have come down to us in the *Aḥadīth*, the complete and multi-ornamented accounts of the life of Prophet Muḥammad (ﷺ), giving us access to an extensive repertoire of supplications.

As Prophet Muḥammad (ﷺ) transmitted, there are basically three ways to receive the answer to a prayer:

1. One receives the answer or the result of the prayer immediately in his life.

2. The prayer is saved for a later, as yet unknown period of one's life.

3.   One receives the answer or result of the prayer in the hereafter (akhirah).

When we pray, we should always keep in mind that the main purpose is not to receive something. The main purpose is to get closer to our Creator. The more we pray and the more our heart become closer to Allah, who is all merciful (SWT).

I hope you enjoy studying and reciting the following supplications. May Allah (SWT) acknowledge our prayers and guide us to the right path.

Salah Moujahed

1

Du'ās of the Prophets
Ādām to Jesus

"Read in the Name of your Lord, Who has created (all that exists."

[Surah Al-'Alaq 96:1]

Du'ā of Ādam:
Repentance and Forgiveness

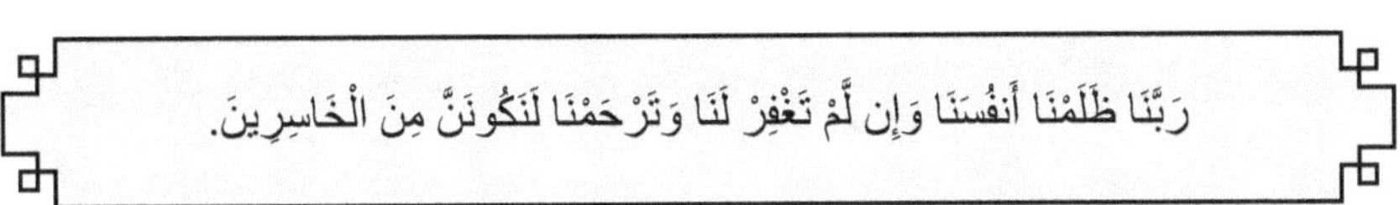

Transliteration:

Rabbanā Ẓalamnā Anfusanā Wa in Lam Taghfir Lanā Wa Tarḥamnā Lanakūnanna Min Al-Khāsirīna.

Translation:

Our Lord! We have wronged ourselves, Unless You forgive us and have mercy on us, we will certainly be losers.

Source: Surah Al-A'rāf 7:23

Duʿā of Noah:
Protection against Defamation

رَبِّ انصُرْنِي بِمَا كَذَّبُونِ

Transliteration:

Rabbi Anṣurnī Bimā Kadhabūni.

Translation:

My Lord, support me because they have denied me.

Source: Surah Al-Muʾminūn 23:26

Du'ā of Noah:
Protection against Infidels and Immoral People

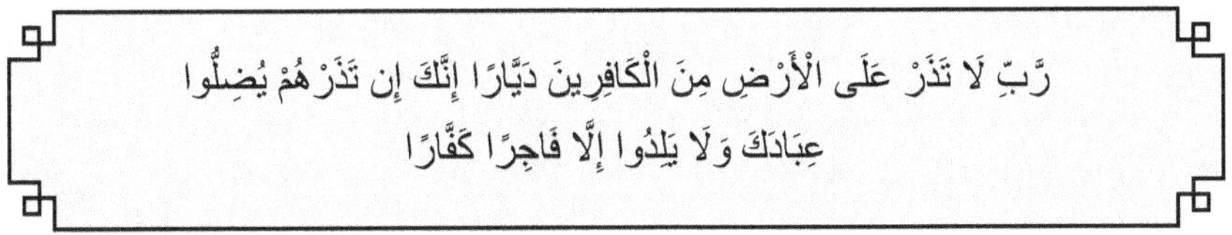

Transliteration:

Rabbi Lā Tadhar 'Ala Al-Arḍi Mina Al-Kāfirīna Dayyārāan innaka in Tadharhum Yuḍillū 'Ibādaka Wa Lā Yalidū Illa Fājiran Kaffāran.

Translation:

My Lord, do not leave of the unbelievers a single dweller on earth. If You leave them, they will mislead your servants, and will breed only wicked unbelievers.

Source: Surah Nūḥ (Noah) 71:26-27

Duʿā of Noah:
Forgiveness of Believers

رَّبِّ اغْفِرْ لِي وَلِوَالِدَيَّ وَلِمَن دَخَلَ بَيْتِيَ مُؤْمِنًا وَلِلْمُؤْمِنِينَ وَالْمُؤْمِنَاتِ وَلَا تَزِدِ الظَّالِمِينَ إِلَّا تَبَارًا

Transliteration:

Rabbi Ighfir Lī Wali-wāli-dayya Wa-limann Dakhala Baītīa Mʿuminan Wa-lilmuʿminīna Wa-lmuʿminīti Wa-Lā-Tazidh Al-ẓalimīna Illa Tabāran.

Translation:

My Lord! Forgive me and my parents, and anyone who enters my home in faith, and all the believing men and believing women; and do not increase the wrongdoers except in perdition.

Source: Surah Nūḥ (Noah) 71:28

Du'ā of Noah:
Mercy

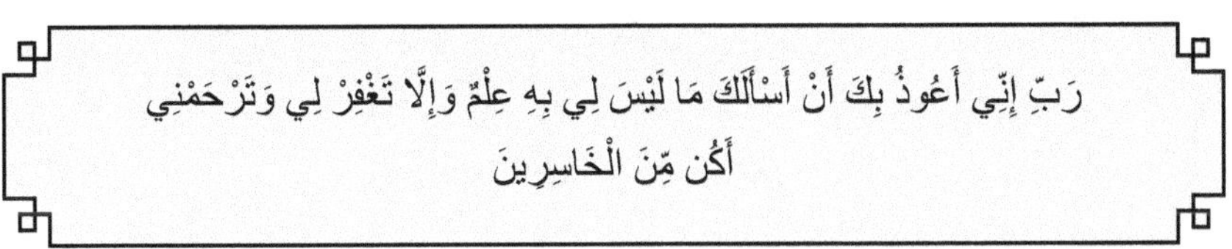

Transliteration:

Rabbi innī 'A'ūdhu Bika An-As'alaka Mā Laysa Lī Bihi 'Ilmun Wa-Illā Taghfir-Lī Wa-Tarḥamnī Akun Mina Al- Khāsirīna.

Translation:

O My Lord, I seek refuge with You, from asking You about what I have no knowledge of. Unless You forgive me, and have mercy on me, I will be one of the losers.

Source: Surah Ḥūd 11:47

Du'ā of Hūd :
Trust in God (Tawakkul)

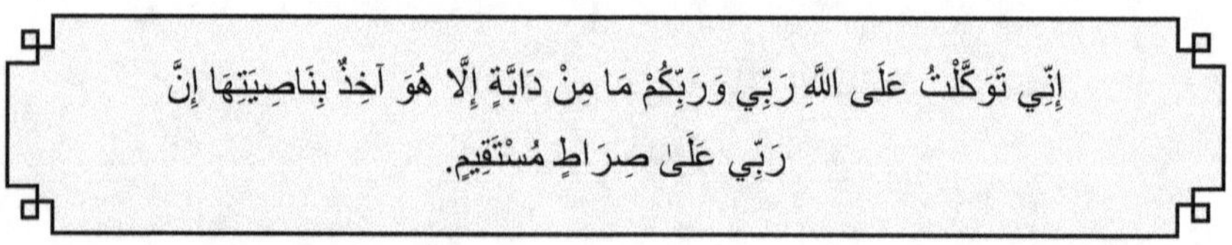

Transliteration:

Innī Tawakkaltu 'Ala Allāhi Rabbī Wa-Rabbikum Mā Min Dābbatin 'Illā Huwa 'Ākhidhun Bināṣīyatihā Inna Rabbī 'Ala Ṣirāṭin Mustaqīmin.

Translation:

I have placed my trust in Allah, my Lord and your Lord. There is not a creature but He holds it by the forelock. My Lord is on a straight path.

Source: Surah Ḥūd 11:56

Du'ā of Abraham:
Security and Subsistence

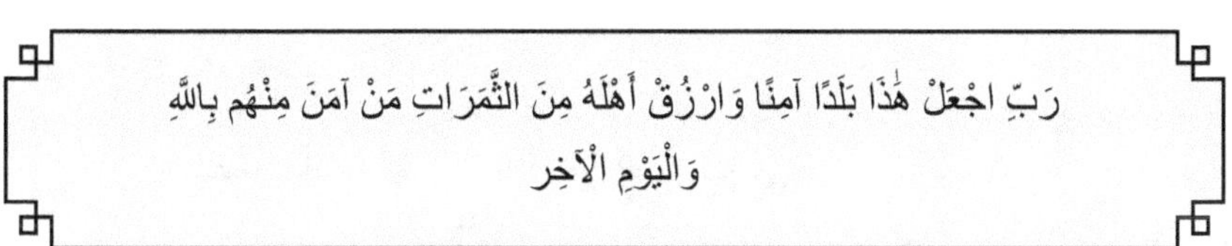

رَبِّ اجْعَلْ هٰذَا بَلَدًا آمِنًا وَارْزُقْ أَهْلَهُ مِنَ الثَّمَرَاتِ مَنْ آمَنَ مِنْهُم بِاللَّهِ وَالْيَوْمِ الْآخِرِ

Transliteration:

Rabbi Aj'al Hādhā Baladāan Āmināan Wa-Rzuq Ahlahu Mina-Athamarāti Man Āmana Minhum Billāhi Wa-Al-Yawmi Al-Ākhiri

Translation:

My Lord! make this a peaceful land, and provide its people with fruits whoever of them believes in Allah and the Last Day.

Source: Surah al-Baqarah 2:126

Du'ā of Abraham:

Intercession for the Family

رَبَّنَا إِنِّي أَسْكَنتُ مِن ذُرِّيَّتِي بِوَادٍ غَيْرِ ذِي زَرْعٍ عِندَ بَيْتِكَ الْمُحَرَّمِ رَبَّنَا لِيُقِيمُوا الصَّلَاةَ فَاجْعَلْ أَفْئِدَةً مِّنَ النَّاسِ تَهْوِي إِلَيْهِمْ وَارْزُقْهُم مِّنَ الثَّمَرَاتِ لَعَلَّهُمْ يَشْكُرُونَ.

Transliteration:

Rabbanā Innī Askantu Min Dhurrīyatī Biwādin Ghaīyri Dhī Zar'in 'Inda Baytīka-l Al-Muḥarrami Rabbanā līyuqīmū Aṣ-Ṣalāata Fāj'al 'Af'idatan Min-An-Nāsi Tahwī ilaīhim Wa-Arzuqhum Mina-Athamarāti L'al allāhum Yashkurūna.

Translation:

Our Lord! I have settled some of my descendants in a barren valley, by Your sacred House (the Ka'bah), our Lord, so that they may perform prayer (Ṣalāt). So make the hearts of (believing) people incline towards them and provide them with fruits, that they will be grateful.

Source: Surah Ibrahim (Abraham) 14:37

Du'ā of Abraham:
Education of Children

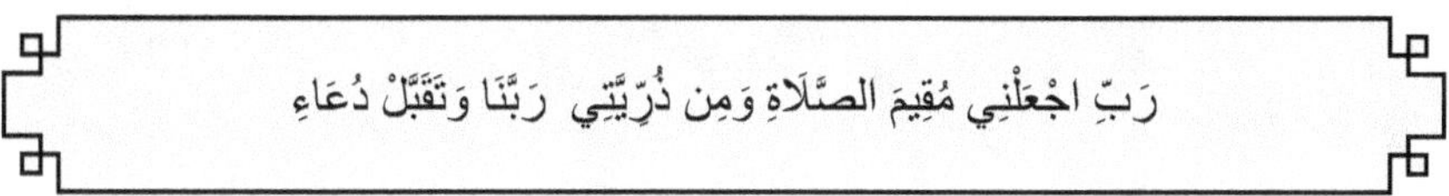

Transliteration:

Rabbi Aj'alnī Muqīma Aṣ-Ṣalāati Wa-Min-Dhurrīyatī, Rabbanā Wa-Taqabbal Du'ā'i.

Translation:

My Lord! Make me one who performs the prayer, and from my offspring. My Lord, accept my supplication.

Source: Surah Ibrahim (Abraham) 14:40

Du'ā of Abraham:

Forgiveness before Judgment Day

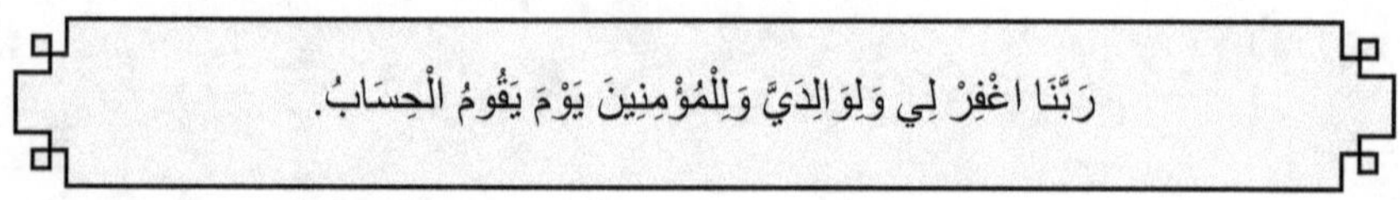

Transliteration:

Rabbanā Aghfir lī Wali-wāli-dayya Wa-lilmu'uminīna Yawma Yaqūmu Al-Ḥisābu.

Translation:

Our Lord! Forgive me, my parents and the believers on the Day of the Reckoning takes place.

Source: Surah Ibrahim (Abraham) 14:41

Du'ā of Abraham:
Desire for a Child

رَبِّ هَبْ لِي مِنَ الصَّالِحِينَ.

Transliteration:

Rabbi Hab Lī Mina Aṣ-Ṣāliḥīna.

Translation:

My Lord! Bless me with righteous offspring.

Source: Surah As-Ṣaffāt 37:100

Du'ā of Abraham:
Wisdom and Truthfulness

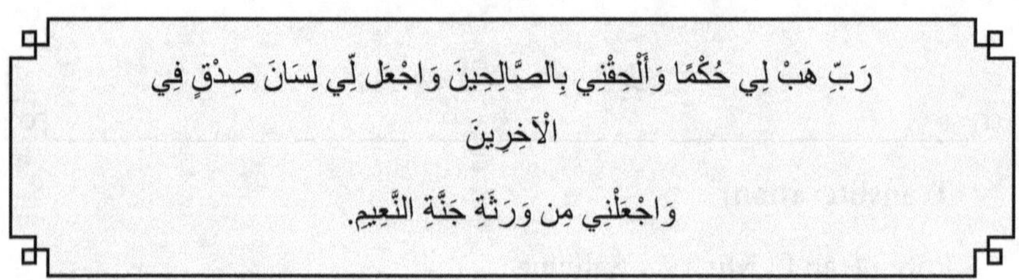

Transliteration:

Rabbi Hab Lī Ḥukmāan Wa-Alḥiqnī Biṣāliḥīna Wa Ajʿal Lī Lisāna Ṣidqin Fī-Al-'Ākhirīna Wa-Ajʿalnī Min-Warathati Jannati An-Naʿīmi.

Translation:

My Lord! Grant me wisdom, and include me with the righteous, And give me a reputation of truth among the others, And make me of the inheritors of the Garden of Bliss.

Source: Surah Ash-Shū'ara 26:83-85

Du'ā of Abraham:
Praise and Forgiveness

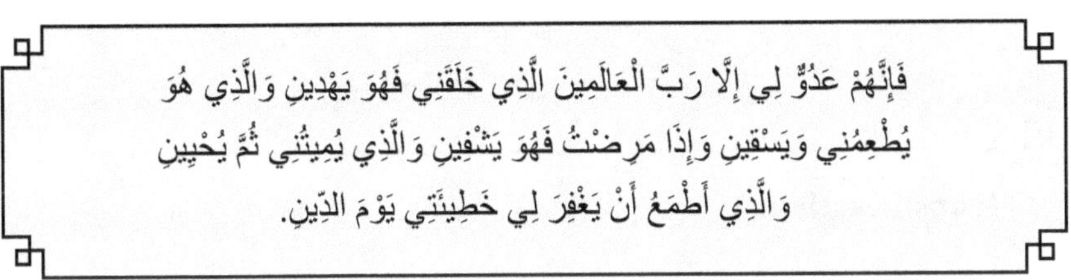

فَإِنَّهُمْ عَدُوٌّ لِي إِلَّا رَبَّ الْعَالَمِينَ الَّذِي خَلَقَنِي فَهُوَ يَهْدِينِ وَالَّذِي هُوَ يُطْعِمُنِي وَيَسْقِينِ وَإِذَا مَرِضْتُ فَهُوَ يَشْفِينِ وَالَّذِي يُمِيتُنِي ثُمَّ يُحْيِينِ وَالَّذِي أَطْمَعُ أَنْ يَغْفِرَ لِي خَطِيئَتِي يَوْمَ الدِّينِ.

Transliteration:

Fā innahum 'Adūwun Lī iIllā Rabba Al-'Ālamīna Al-Ladhī Khalaqanī Fuhuwa Yahdīni Wa-Al-Ladhī Huwa Yuṭ'imūnī Wa-Yasqīni Wa-idhā Mariḍtu Fuhuwa Yashfīni Wa Al-Ladhī Yumītunī Thumma Yuḥyīni Wa Al-Ladhī 'Aṭma'u 'An Yaghfira Lī Khaṭī'atī Yauwma Ad-Dīni.

Translation:

They are enemies to me, but not so the Lord of the Worlds. He who created me, and guides me, He who feeds me, and waters me, And when I get sick, He heals me, He who makes me die, and then revives me. He who, I hope, will forgive my sins on the Day of the Reckoning

Source: Surah Ash-Shū'ara 26:77-82

Du'ā of Lūt (Lot):
Help Against Evildoers

رَبِّ انْصُرْنِي عَلَى الْقَوْمِ الْمُفْسِدِينَ.

Transliteration:

Rabbi Anṣurnī 'Ala Al-Qawm-i Al-Mufsidīna.

Translation:

My Lord! Help me against these mischievous people.

Source: Surah Al-'Ankabut 29:30

Du'ā of Lūt (Lot):
Rescue from Aggressors

رَبِّ نَجِّنِي وَأَهْلِي مِمَّا يَعْمَلُونَ

Transliteration:

Rabbi Najjinī Wa Ahlī Mimmā Ya'malūna.

Translation:

My Lord! Save me and my family from what they are doing.

Source: Surah Ash-Shū'ara 26:169

Duʿā of Shuaib:
Justice

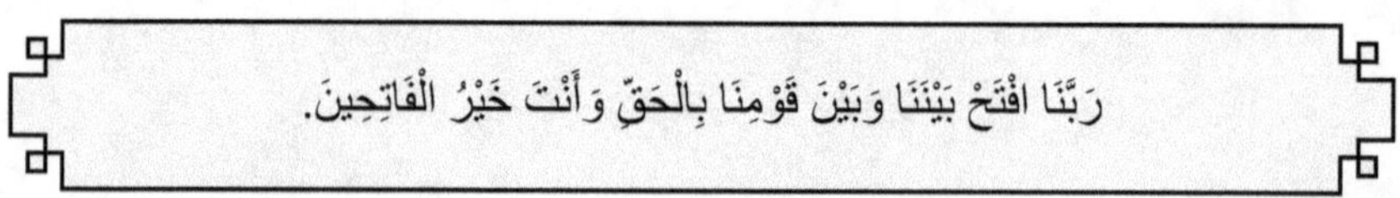

Transliteration:

Rabbanā Aftaḥ Baīnanā Wa-Baīna Qawminā Bil-Ḥaqqi Wa Anta Khaīru Al-Fātiḥīna.

Translation:

O Lord, decide between us and our people in truth, for You are the Best of Deciders.

Source: Surah Al-ʿĀrāf 7:89

Du'ā of Yūsūf (Joseph):
Grief and Suffering

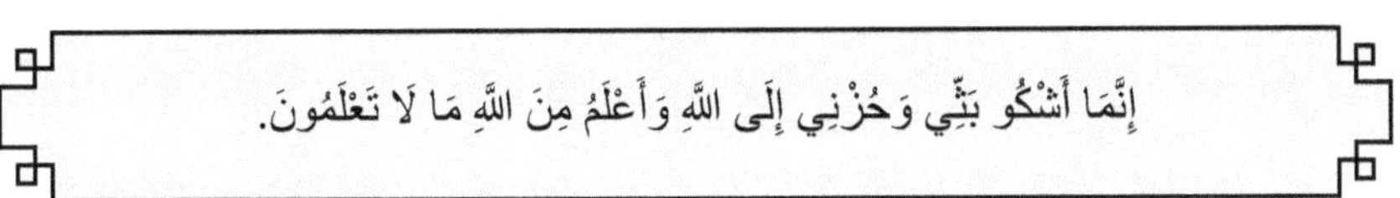

Transliteration:

Innamā Ashkū Bathī Wa Ḥuznī illa'l -Allāhi Wa-Ā'lamu Mina-l Allāhi Mā Lā Ta'lamūna.

Translation:

I complain of my grief and sorrow only to Allah, and I know from Allah what you do not know.

Source: Surah Yūsūf (Joseph) 12:86

Du'ā of Yūsuf (Joseph):
Recognition in the Hereafter

رَبِّ قَدْ آتَيْتَنِي مِنَ الْمُلْكِ وَعَلَّمْتَنِي مِنْ تَأْوِيلِ الْأَحَادِيثِ ۚ فَاطِرَ السَّمَاوَاتِ وَالْأَرْضِ أَنْتَ وَلِيِّي فِي الدُّنْيَا وَالْآخِرَةِ ۖ تَوَفَّنِي مُسْلِمًا وَأَلْحِقْنِي بِالصَّالِحِينَ.

Transliteration:

Rabbi Qad 'Ātaytanī Mina-l Al-Mulki Wa 'Allamtanī Min T'awīli Al-'Aḥādīthi Fāṭira As-Samāwāti Wa Al-Arḍi Anta Walīyi Fī-Ad-Dunyā Wa Al-Ākhirati Tawaffanī Muslimāan Wa 'Alḥiqnī Biṣāliḥīna.

Translation:

My Lord! You have given me power and taught me the interpretation of dreams. Originator of the heavens and the earth! You are my Guardian in this world and in the Hereafter. Make me die to faith and join the righteous.

Source: Surah Yūsuf (Joseph)12:101

Du'ā of Ayyūb (Job):
Support in Misfortune

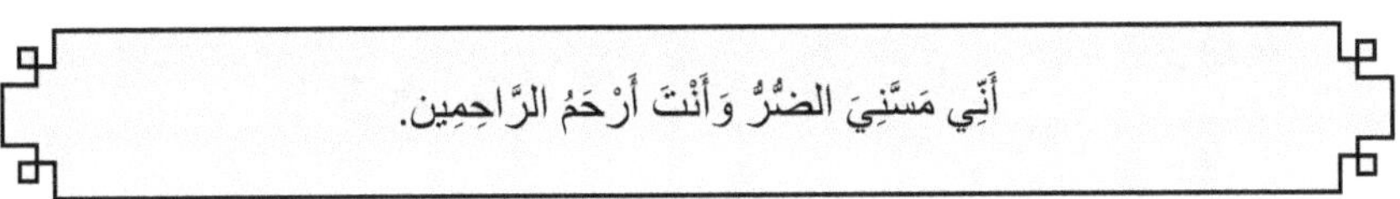

Transliteration:

Annī Massanī Aḍ-Ḍurru Wa Anta Arḥamu-r Ar-Rāḥimīna.

Translation:

Great harm has afflicted me, and you are the Most Merciful of the merciful.

Source: Surah Al 'Anbīyā' 21:83

Duʿā of Yunūs:
Praise

لَّا إِلَهَ إِلَّا أَنتَ سُبْحَانَكَ إِنِّي كُنتُ مِنَ الظَّالِمِينَ.

Transliteration:

Lā ilāha illa Anta Subḥānaka innī Kuntu Mina Aẓ-Ẓālimīna.

Translation:

There is no god except You. Glory be to You! I was one of the Wrongdoers.

Source: Surah Al-'Anbīyā' 21:87

Duʿā of Moses:
Forgiveness

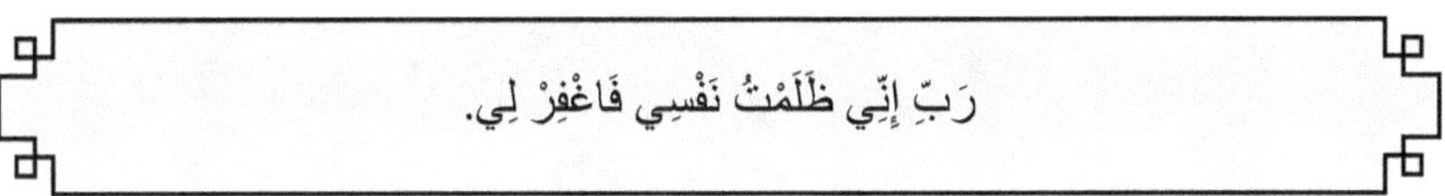

Transliteration:

Rabbi innī Ẓalamtu Nafsī Fāghfir Lī.

Translation:

My Lord! I have wronged my soul, so forgive me.

Source: Surah Al-Qaṣaṣ 28:16

Duʿā of Moses:
Rizq (Subsistance)

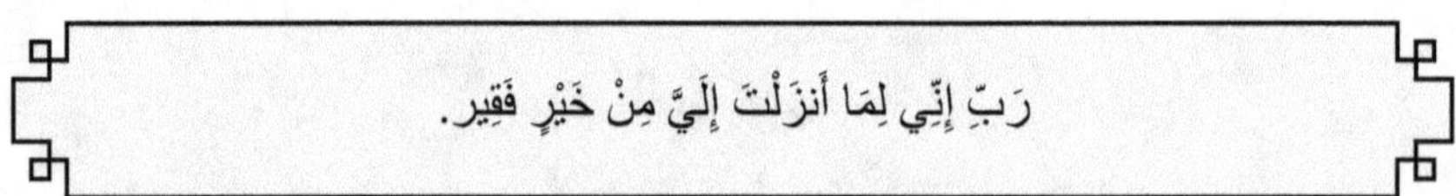

Transliteration:

Rabbi innī limā Anzalta Ilaīyya Min Khaīyrin Faqīrun.

Translation:

My Lord! I am in (desperate) need of all the good that You send down for me.

Source: Surah Al- Qaṣaṣ 28:24

Du'ā of Moses:
Protection from Wrongdoing People

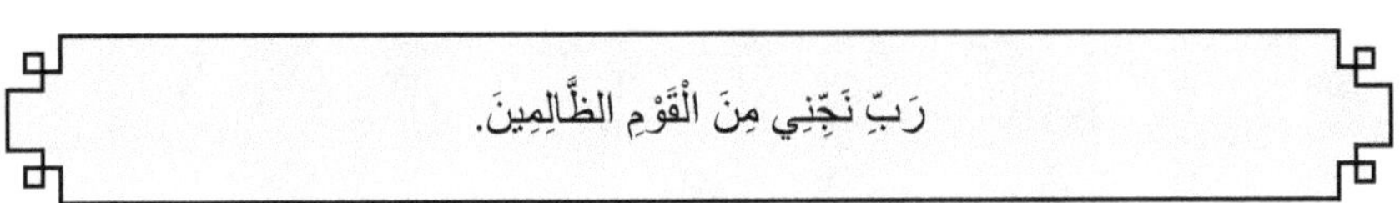

Transliteration:

Rabbi Najjinī Mina Al-Qawmi Aẓ-Ẓālimīna.

Translation:

My Lord! Deliver me from the wrongdoing people!

Source: Surah Al- Qaṣaṣ 28:21

Du'ā of Moses:
Repentance and Return to Allah

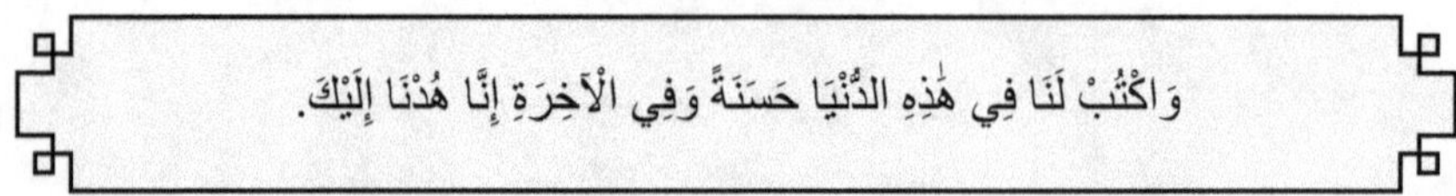

Transliteration:

Wa-Aktub Lanā Fī Hadhihi Ad-Dunyā Ḥasanatan Wa Fī Al-Ākhirati innā Hudnā Ilaīyka.

Translation:

And inscribe for us goodness in this world, and in the Hereafter.

Source: Surah Al-'Ārāf 7:156

Du'ā of Moses:
Lose Fear in Public Speaking

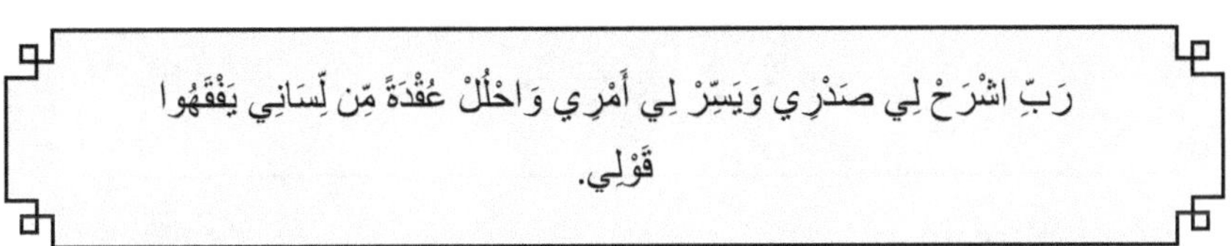

Transliteration:

Rabbi Ashraḥ Lī Ṣadrī Wa-Yassir Lī Amrī Wa-Aḥlul 'Uqdatan Min Lisanī Yafqahu Qawlī.

Translation:

My Lord! put my heart at peace for me, and ease my task for me, And untie the knot from my tongue, So they can understand my speech.

Source: Surah Ṭaha 20:25-28

Duʻā of Moses:
Turning away from Criminals

رَبِّ بِمَا أَنْعَمْتَ عَلَيَّ فَلَنْ أَكُونَ ظَهِيرًا لِّلْمُجْرِمِينَ

Transliteration:

Rabbi Bimā Anʻamta ʻAlayya Falan Akūna Ẓahīrāan lil-mujrimīna.

Translation:

My Lord! For all Your favors upon me, I will never be supporter of the criminals.

Source: Surah Al-Qaṣaṣ 28:17

Du'ā of Dawūd (David):
Patience and Firmness

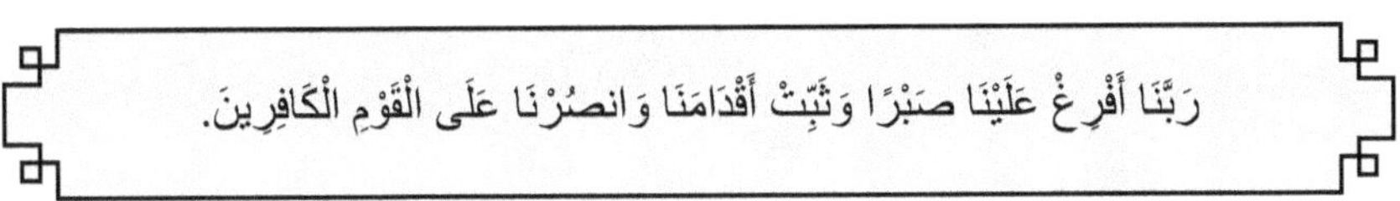

Transliteration:

Rabbanā Afrigh ʿAlaīynā Ṣabrāan Wa-Thabbit Aqdāmanā Wa-Anṣurnā ʿAlá Al-Qawmi Al-Kāfirīna.

Translation:

Our Lord! pour down patience on us, and strengthen our foothold, and support us against the faithless people.

Source: Al-Baqarah 2:250

Du'ā of Sulaimān (Salomon):
Responsibility for Leadership

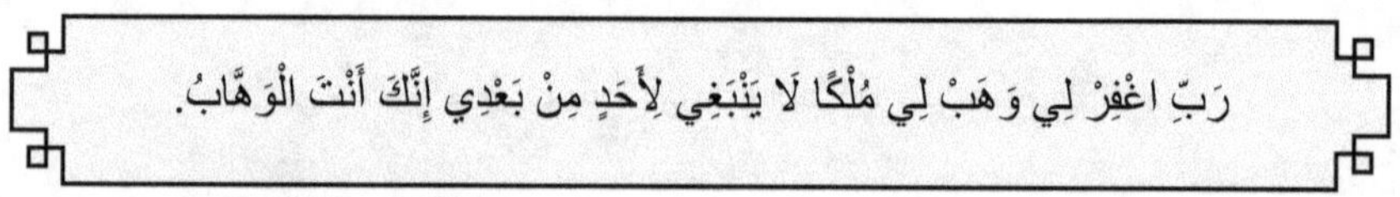

Transliteration:

Rabbi Aghfir lī Wa-hab lī Mulkāan lā Yanbaghī li-aḥadin Min Ba'dī Innaka Anta Al-Wahhābu.

Translation:

My Lord! forgive me, and grant me a kingdom never to be attained by anyone after me. You are the Giver (of all bounties).

Source: Surah Ṣād 38:35

Du'ā of Sulaimān (Salomon):
Recognition

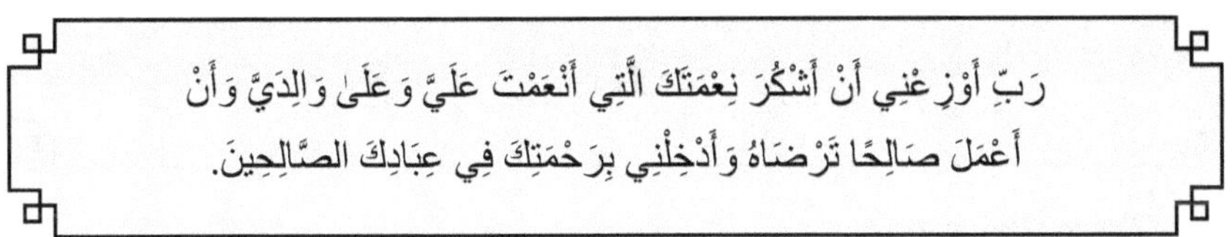

Transliteration:

Rabbi awzi'nī An Ash-koura Ni'mataka Al-latī An'amta 'Alaīyya Wa-'Ala wa-lidaīyya Wa An-A'mala Ṣāliḥāan Tarḍāhou Wa Adkhilnī Biraḥmatika Fī Ibādika Aṣ-Ṣāliḥīna.

Translation:

My Lord, direct me to be thankful for the blessings you have bestowed upon me and upon my parents, and to do good works that please You. And admit me, by Your grace, into the company of Your virtuous servants.

Source: Surah Al-Naml 27:19

Duʿā of Zakarīyah (Zachariah):
Solitude and Childlessness

رَبِّ لَا تَذَرْنِي فَرْدًا وَأَنْتَ خَيْرُ الْوَارِثِينَ

Transliteration:

Rabbi lā Tadharnī Fardāan Wa-anta Khaīyru Al-Wārithīna.

Translation:

My Lord! Do not leave me alone, even though You are the Best of heirs.

Source: Surah Al-ʿAnbīyaʾ 21:89

Du'ā of Zakarīyah (Zachariah):
Righteous Offspring

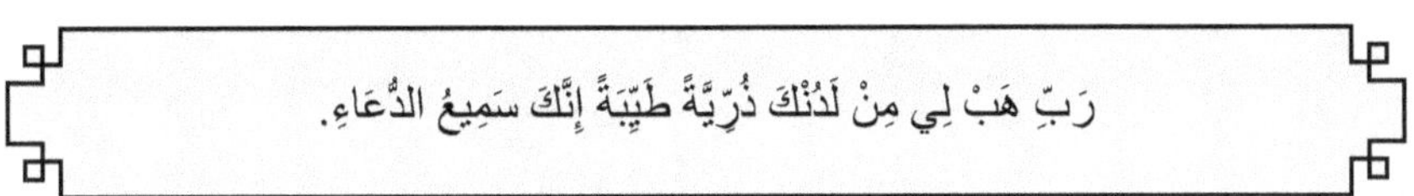

Transliteration:

Rabbi Hab lī Min ladunka Dhurrīyatan Ṭaīyyibatan innaka Samīʿuw Ad-Duʿāʾi.

Translation:

My Lord! Grant me by Your Grace righteous offspring, for You are certainly the Hearer of (all) prayers.

Source: Surah Al-ʿImrān 3:38

Du'ā of Jesus :
Rizq (Subsistence)

اللَّهُمَّ رَبَّنَا أَنْزِلْ عَلَيْنَا مَائِدَةً مِنَ السَّمَاءِ تَكُونُ لَنَا عِيدًا لِأَوَّلِنَا وَآخِرِنَا وَآيَةً مِنْكَ وَارْزُقْنَا وَأَنْتَ خَيْرُ الرَّازِقِينَ.

Transliteration:

Allāhumma Rabbanā Anzil 'Alaynā Mā'idatan Mina As-Samā'i Takūnu Lanā 'Īdāan Li-Awwalinā Wa-Ākhirinā Wa-Āyatan Minka Wa-Arzuqnā Wa-Anta Khaīyru Ar-Rāziqīna.

Translation:

O Allah, our Lord! Send us from heaven a table spread with food as a banquet for us – for the first and last of us – as a sign from You. And provide for us! You are indeed the Best Providers.

Source: Surah Al-Mā'idah 5:114

Du'ā of Jesus:
Overcoming Anger

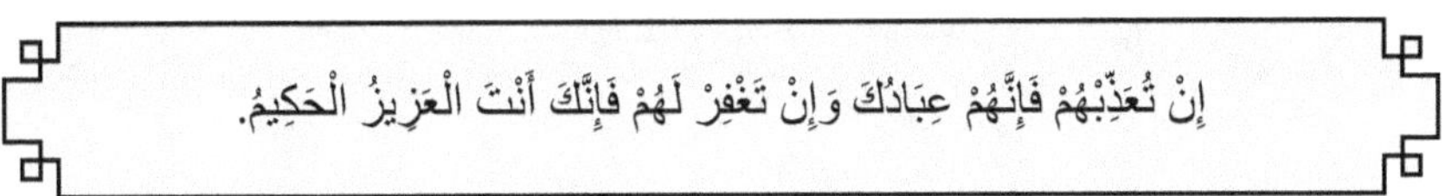

إِنْ تُعَذِّبْهُمْ فَإِنَّهُمْ عِبَادُكَ وَإِنْ تَغْفِرْ لَهُمْ فَإِنَّكَ أَنْتَ الْعَزِيزُ الْحَكِيمُ.

Transliteration:

In Tu'adhibhum Fā-Innahum 'Ibāduka Wa-in-taghfir lahum fā-innaka anta Al-'Azīzu Al-Ḥakīmu.

Translation:

If You punish them, they are your servants; but if You forgive them, You are surely the Almighty, All-Wise.

Source: Al-Mā'idah 5:118

Part

2

Du'ās of Prophet Muhammad ﷺ

For Love

اللَّهُمَّ إِنِّي أَسْأَلُكَ فِعْلَ الْخَيْرَاتِ، وَتَرْكَ الْمُنْكَرَاتِ، وَحُبَّ الْمَسَاكِينِ، وَأَنْ تَغْفِرَ لِي، وَتَرْحَمَنِي، وَإِذَا أَرَدْتَ فِتْنَةَ قَوْمٍ فَتَوَفَّنِي غَيْرَ مَفْتُونٍ، وَأَسْأَلُكَ حُبَّكَ وَحُبَّ مَنْ يُحِبُّكَ، وَحُبَّ عَمَلٍ يُقَرِّبُنِي إِلَى حُبِّكَ.

Transliteration:

Allāhumma innī As-aluka fiʻla al-khaīrāt wa Tarka al-munkarāt wa-Ḥubba al-masākīn wa-an-taghfira lī wa-Tarḥamanī. Wa-idha arad-ta fitnata qawmin fa-tawaffanī ghayra maftun. Wa as-aluka Ḥubbak wa-Ḥubba man yuḥibbuk wa-Ḥubba ʻamalin yuqarribuni ila Ḥubbika.

Translation:

O Allah! I ask of you the doing of the good deeds, avoiding the evil deeds, loving the poor, and that You forgive me, and have mercy upon me. And when You have willed Fitnah in the people, then take me without the Fitnah. And I ask You for Your love, the love of whomever You love, and the love of the deeds that bring one nearer to Your love.

Source: Jāmʻi At-Tirmidhī 5/369

Mercy in Adversity

اللهمَّ إليك أشكو ضَعْفَ قوَّتي، وقلةَ حيلتي، وهواني على الناس، يا أرحَمَ الراحِمِينَ، أنت رَبُّ المستضعَفِينَ، وأنت ربِّي، إلى مَن تَكِلُني؟ إلى بعيدٍ يَتجهَّمُني، أو إلى عدوٍّ ملَّكْتَهُ أمري، إن لم يكُنْ بك غضَبٌ عليَّ فلا أُبالي، غيرَ أن عافيتَك هي أوسَعُ لي، أعُوذُ بنورِ وجهِك الذي أشرَقتْ له الظُّلماتُ، وصلَح عليه أمرُ الدُّنيا والآخرةِ، أن يَحِلَّ عليَّ غضَبُك، أو أن يَنزلَ بي سخَطُك، لك العُتْبى حتى ترضى، ولا حولَ ولا قوَّةَ إلا بك.

Transliteration:

Allāhumma ilaīka ashku Ḍhafa Quwatī, wa Qillata Ḥihlatī, wa-hawānī ʿala al-Nāsi, yā arḥama ar-Raḥimīna, anta Rabbu al-Mustaḍafīna, wa ʿanta Rabbī, ila man Takilunī? ila baʿiden yata-jahumnī, awu ila ʿaduwin Mallaktahu amrī, in lam yakun bika Ghaḍabun ʿalaya falā ubālī, Ghaīyra anna ʿĀfīyataka hiya au-saʿū lī, aʿudhu binuri wajhika al-adhī ashraqat lahu aẓ-Ẓulumāt, wa Ṣalaḥa ʿalaīhi amru ad-dunīya wa'l Ākhirati, an yaḥilla ʿalaya Ghaḍabuka, aw an yanzila bī Sakhaṭuka, laka'l ʿŪtba Ḥatta Tarḍa, wa-lā Ḥawla wa-lā Quwata illa bika.

Translation:

O Allah, (only) to You I complain of my weakness, my lack of resourcefulness, and my humiliation over people, O Most Merciful of the merciful, You are the Lord of the weak, and You are my Lord. To whom do you leave me? To a far away scorn me, or to an enemy to whom You give power over me?

If You are not angry with me, then I do not care, but Your well-being is broader for me, I seek refuge in the light of Your face for which the darkness has risen. And the wrath of the hereafter will be set right by me. You have the blame until you are satisfied, and there is no might or might but with You.

Source: Ṣaḥīḥ Muslim

Protection Against Evil

أَعوذُ بِكَلِماتِ اللهِ التّامّاتِ، الّتي لا يُجاوِزُهُنَّ بَرٌّ ولا فاجِرٌ، مِن شرِّ ما خلقَ، وذرأَ، وبرأَ، ومِن شرِّ ما ينزلُ مِن السَّماءِ، ومِن شرِّ ما يعرُجُ فيها، ومِن شرِّ ما ذرأَ في الأرضِ، ومِن شرِّ ما يَخرجُ مِنها، ومِن شرِّ فِتَنِ اللَّيلِ والنَّهارِ، ومِن شرِّ كلِّ طارقٍ يطرُقُ، إلَّا طارقًا يطرقُ بِخَيرٍ، يا رَحمانُ.

Transliteration:

A'ūdhu bi-kalimāti Allāhi atāmāti, al-latī lā yū-Jawizūhunna barrun wa lā fājirun, min sharri mā khallaqa, wa-dharrā'a, wa-barra'a, wa min shari mā yunzilu min as-samā'i, wa min shari ma y'aruju fīha, wa min shari mā dhara'a fī'l arḍhi wa min shari ma yakhruju min hā, wa min shari fitani al-laīyli wan-nāhari, wa min sharri qulli Ṭāriqin yaṭrūqu, illā Ṭāriqan yaṭruqu bi-khaīyrin, yā Raḥmān.

Translation:

I seek refuge in the perfect words of God, which neither the righteous nor the wicked can pass, from the evil of what He created, spurted, and healed, and from the evil of what descends from the sky, and from the evil of what ascends in it, and from the evil of what comes out of the earth and what comes out of it. The temptations of night and day, and from the evil of every Tarek knocks, except for a Tariq who knocks with good, O Most Merciful.

Source: Al Albānī, Imām Mālik 2/901

Remorse and Forgiveness

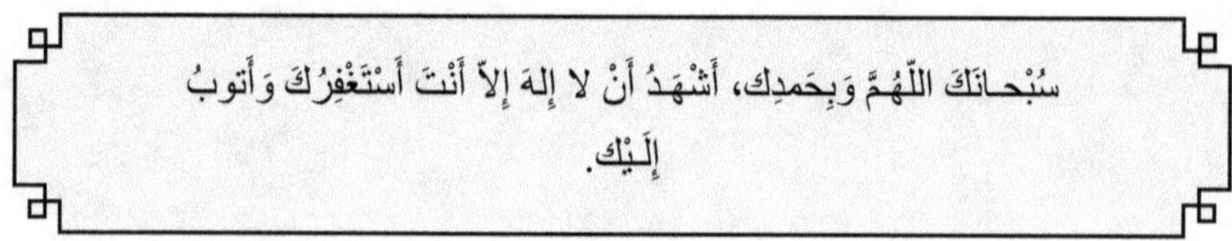

Transliteration:

Subḥānāka Allāhumma wa bi-ḥamdika, Ash-hadu Ann lā ilaha illā Anta, Astaghfiruka wa Atubu ilaīyka.

Translation:

The glory is Yours, O Allah, and the praise is Yours. I bear witness that there is none worthy of worship but Thee. I seek Your forgiveness and repent to You.

Source: Abu Dawūd 4859

Full Protection

اللَّهُمَّ إِنِّي أَسْأَلُك العافيةَ في الدُّنيا والآخرةِ اللَّهمَّ أسألُك العفوَ والعافيةَ في ديني ودنيايَ وأهلي ومالي اللَّهمَّ استر عوراتي وآمِن رَوعاتي اللَّهمَّ احفظني من بينِ يدىَّ ومن خَلفي وعن يَميني وعَن شِمالي ومن فَوقي وأعوذُ بعظَمتِك أن اغتالَ من تحتي.

Transliteration:

Allāhumma innī as-aluka al'afīyata fī ad-dunīya wal-Ākhīra. Allāhumma as-aluka'l-'afwa wa'l 'afīata fī dīnī wa-dunyāya wa-ahlī wa-malī. Allāhumma Astir 'Aurātī wa-Āmin Rau'ātī. Allāhumma aḥfadhnī min baīni yadaya wa-min Khalfī wa 'an yamīnī wa 'an shimālī wa min fawqī wa a'ūdhu bi-'Aẓamatika an ughtala min taḥtī.

Translation:

O Allah! I ask Thee for forgiveness and security in my religion and my worldly affairs, in my family and my property; O Allah! conceal my fault or faults (according to Uthman's version), and keep me safe from the things which I fear; O Allah! guard me in front of me and behind me, on my right hand and on my left, and from above me: and I seek in Thy greatness from receiving unexpected harm from below me.

Source: Abu Dawūd 5074

Healing

اللهمّ رَبَّ النَّاسِ أَذْهِبِ البَاسَ، واشْفِ أَنْتَ الشَّافِي، لا شِفَاءَ إِلَّا شِفَاؤُكَ، شِفَاءً لا يُغَادِرُ سَقَمًا.

Transliteration:

Allāhumma Rabba An-Nās Adhhib Al-b'as, washfi anta al-ashāfī, lā shifā'a illa shifā'uka, shifā'an lā yughādiru saqaman.

Translation:

O Allah, Lord of mankind, take away the pain, and heal, You are the Healer, there is no cure but Your healing, a cure that does not leave sickness.

Source: Al Bukhārī with Al-Fatḥ 10/206 and Muslim 4/1721

Protection in this World and the Hereafter

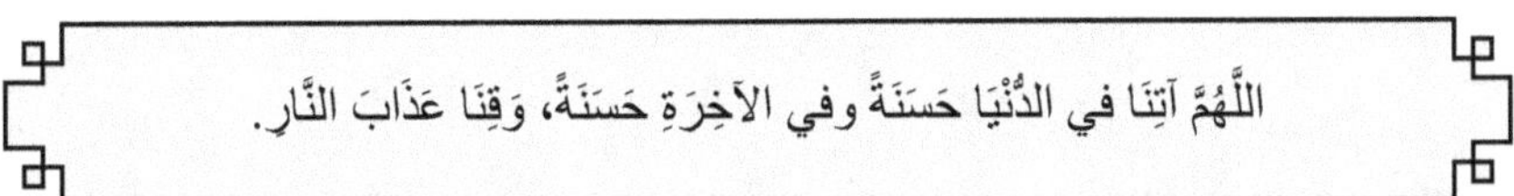

Transliteration:

Allāhumma Ātina fī al-dunīyā Ḥasanatan wa fī al-Ākhirati Ḥasanatan, wa-qinā 'Adhāba al-Nāri.

Translation:

O Allah, give us good in this world and good in the hereafter, and save us from the torment of the fire.

Source: Surah Al-Baqarah 2:201

Guidance and Independence

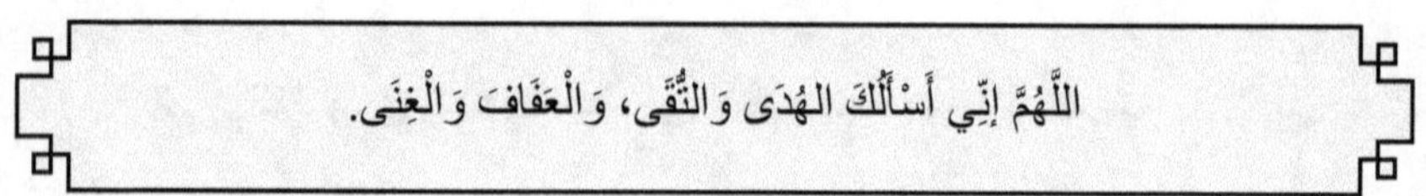

Transliteration:

Allāhumma innī As'aluka al-huda' waltuqa', wal 'Afāfa wal-Ghina'.

Translation:

O Allah, I ask you for guidance, righteousness, chastity, and independence.

Source: Ṣaḥīḥ Muslim 2721

Motivation in Times of Crisis

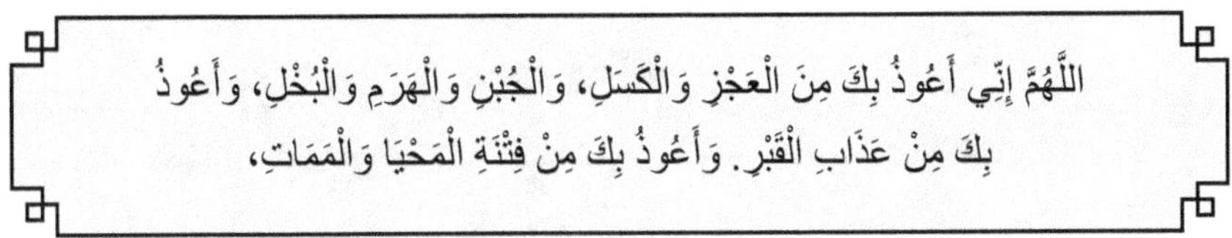

Transliteration:

Allāhumma innī a'ūdhu bika min-al-'Ajzi wal-kassali, wal Jubni wal-harami wal-būkhli, wa a'ūdhu bika min 'adhāba al-qabri, wa min fitnati al-maḥyā wal mamāti.

Translation:

O Allah! I seek refuge with You from helplessness, laziness, cowardice and feeble old age; I seek refuge with You from afflictions of life and death and seek refuge with You from the punishment in the grave.

Source: Sahih al-Bukhārī 2823

Eliminate Sorrows and Worries

اللَّهُمَّ إِنِّي عَبْدُكَ، ابْنُ عَبْدِكَ، ابْنُ أَمَتِكَ، نَاصِيَتِي بِيَدِكَ، مَاضِي فِيَّ حُكْمُكَ، عَدْلٌ فِيَّ قَضَاؤُكَ، أَسْأَلُكَ بِكُلِّ اسْمٍ هُوَ لَكَ سَمَّيْتَ بِهِ نَفْسَكَ، أَوْ أَنْزَلْتَهُ فِي كِتَابِكَ، أَوْ عَلَّمْتَهُ أَحَدًا مِنْ خَلْقِكَ، أَوِ اسْتَأْثَرْتَ بِهِ فِي عِلْمِ الْغَيْبِ عِنْدَكَ، أَنْ تَجْعَلَ الْقُرْآنَ رَبِيعَ قَلْبِي، وَنُورَ صَدْرِي، وَجَلَاءَ حُزْنِي، وَذَهَابَ هَمِّي

Transliteration:

Allāhumma innī 'abduka ibni 'abdika, ibni ammatika, naṣiatī bīyadika, māḍīn fī Ḥukmuka, 'Adlun fī qaḍā'uka. as'aluka bi-kuli ismin hua laka samaīta bihi nafsuka, auw Anzaltahu fī kitābika, auw 'allamtahu aḥadann min khalqika, au istatharta bihi fī 'ilmi al-ghaībi 'indaka. An taj'ala al-qur'āna rabīa' qalbī, wanura Ṣadrī, wajala'a Ḥuznī, wa-dhahāba hammī.

Translation:

O God, I am Your servant, the son of Your servant, the son of Your handmaid, and at Your disposal; my forelock is in Your hand; Your judgment is effective regarding me; just concerning me is Your decree; I ask You by every name You hast by which You hast called Yourself, or sent down in Your Book, or taught any of Your creatures, or kept to Yourself in the hidden place of the unseen, to make the Qur'an the Spring of my heart and the means of clearing away my care and grief.

Source: Aḥmed 3712

Assistance and Support

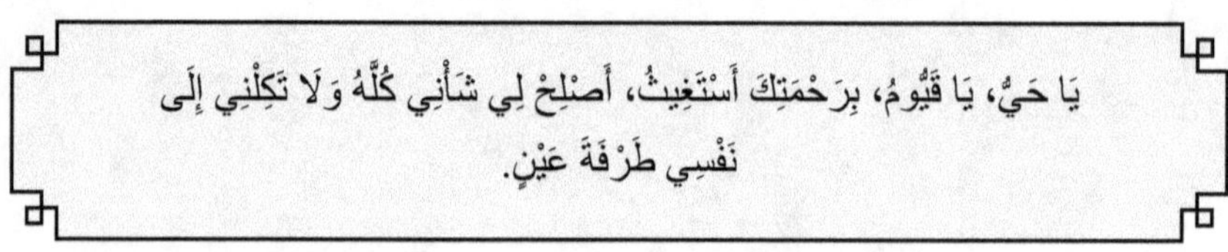

Transliteration:

Yā Ḥayyu yā Qayyūm, bi raḥmatika astaghīth, aṣliḥ lī sha'nī kullahu, wa lā takilanī ila nafsī Ṭarfata 'Aīayn.

Translation:

O Ever-Living, O Self-Subsisting and Supporter of all, in Your mercy I seek relief. Rectify my affairs, all of them, and do not entrust me to myself even for the blink of an eye.

Source: Al-Albāni 1:273

Depressions

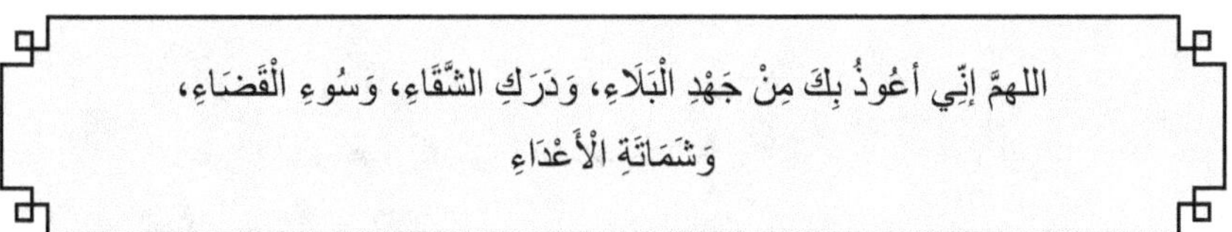

Transliteration:

Allāhumma innī a'ūdhu bika min Jahdi al-balā', wa-daraki al-shaqā', wa-sua' alqaḍā', wa-shāmatati al'ada'.

Translation:

O Allah, I seek refuge in You from the effort of affliction, the realization of misery, a bad judgment, and the gloating of enemies.

Source: Abū Huraīyrah 7/1471

Subsistence (Rizq) / Emergency Care

اللّهم ارزقني رزقًا واسعًا حلالًا طيّبًا من غير كدّ، واستجب دعائي من غير ردّ، وأعوذ بكَ من الفضيحتين الفقر والدّين، اللّهم يا رزاق السائلين، يا راحم المساكين، ويا ذا القوة المتين، ويا خير الناصرين، يا ولي المؤمنين، يا غيّاث المستغيثين، إياك نعبد وإيّاك نستعين، اللّهم إن كان رزقي في السماء فأنزله وإن كان رزقي في الأرض فأخرجه وإن كان بعيدًا فقرّبه وإن كان قريبًا فيسره وإن كان كثيرًا فبارك فيه يا أرحم الراحمين.

Transliteration:

Allāhumma Ar-zuknī Rizqan Was'ian Ḥalalan Ṭaība Min Ghaīri Kaddin, Wastajibb Du'āī Min Ghaīri Raddin Wa a'ūdhu Bika Min Al faḍīhataīni Al-faqru Wad-dīyni, Allāhumma Yā Razāq As-sā'Ilīna, Yā Rāḥim Al-Massākīni, Wa yā Dhā Al-quwati Al-matīni, Wa yā Khaīra An-naṣirīna, Yā Walī Al-Mu'minīna, Ya Ghaīātha Al-Mustaghīthīna, 'iyyāka N'abūdu Wa'iyyāka Nasta'īnu. Allāhumma in Kāna Rizqā Fā Assamā'i Fā'anzilhu Wa in Kāna Rizkī Fi Al'Arḍi Fā'akhrijhu Wa in Kāna Ba'idan Fakarribhu Wa in Kāna Qarība Fa-yassirhu Wa in Kāna Kathīran Fabārik Fīhi Yā Arḥama Ar-Raḥimīna.

Translation:

O Allah, grant me a vast, lawful and good sustenance without toil, and answer my supplications without being rejected. I seek refuge in You from the two scandals, poverty and debt.

O Allah, O Provider of the beggar, O Merciful of the poor, O Possessor of firm strength, O Best of Helpers, O Guardian of the Faithful, O Helper of those who seek help, Beware of worship and Thine aid we seek.

O Allah, if my sustenance is in the sky, then send it down. And if my sustenance is in the earth, then bring it out. And if it is far, then bring it close. And if it is near, then make it easy. And if it is much, then bless it. O Allah, the Most Merciful.

Source: Anas ibn Mālik

Useful Knowledge

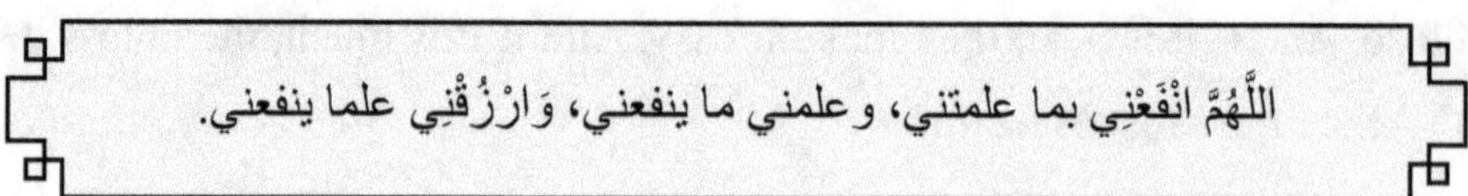

Transliteration:

Allāhumma anfaʿnī bimā ʿallamtanī, wa ʿallimnī mā yanfaʿunī, warzūqnī ʿilmān yanfaʿunī.

Translation:

O Allah, benefit me with what You have taught me, and teach me that which will benefit me, and give me knowledge that will benefit me.

Source: Sunan At-Tirmidhī 3599

Refuge from Evil

اللهم لكَ الحمدُ كالذي نقولُ وخيرًا ممَّا نقولُ، اللهم لكَ صلاتي ونُسُكي ومَحْياي ومَماتي، وإليكَ مآبي، ولكَ ربِّ تُراثي، اللهم إنِّي أعوذُ بكَ مِن عذابِ القبرِ، ووَسْوَسةِ الصدرِ، وشَتاتِ الأمرِ، اللهم إنِّي أعوذُ بكَ مِن شرِّ ما تجيءُ به الريحُ.

Transliteration:

Allāhumma laka al-Ḥamdu kalladhī naqulu wa-khaīran mimmā naqulu. Allāhumma laka Ṣalātī wa-Nūssukī wa-Maḥyaīy wa-Mamātī, wa ilaīka ma'ābī, wa laka Rabbi Turathī, Allāhumma innī a'ūdhu bika min 'adābill Qabri, wa was-wasati as-Ṣadri, wa-Shatāti al'amri. Allāhumma innī a'ūdhu bika min sharri mā-Taji'u bihi ar-Riḥu.

Translation:

O Allah, praise be to you as what we say and better than what we say. O Allah, to You is my prayer, my sacrifice, my life and my death, and to You is my hope, and to You is the Lord of my legacy. O Allah, I seek refuge in You from the torment of the grave, from the turmoil of the chest, and from the scattering of affairs. Oh Allah, I seek refuge in You from the evil of what the wind brings.

Source: Sunan At-Tirmidhī 3520

Relief in Life

اللهم يا ذا الرحمة الواسعة، يا مُطَّلِعاً على السرائر والضمائر
والهواجس والخواطر، لا يعزب عنك شيء، أسألك فيضة من فيضان
فضلك، وقبضة من نور سلطانك، وأُنسًا وفرجاً من بحر كرمك، أنت
بيدك الأمر كلّه ومقاليد كل شيء، فهب لنا ما تقرّ به أعيننا، وتُغنينا
عن سؤال غيرك، فإنك واسع الكرم، كثير الجود، حسن الشيم، في
بابك واقفون، ولجودك الواسع المعروف منتظرون، يا كريم يا رحيم.

Transliteration:

Allāhumma Yā Dha Ar-Raḥmati Al-Wasi'ati, Yā Muṭali'an 'Ala As-Sarā'iri Wa-Ḍhamā'iri Wal-Hawājisi Wal-Khawaṭiri, Lā Ya'zūbu 'anka Shaī'un, As'aluka Faīḍatan Min Faīḍāni Faḍlika, Wa-Qabḍatan Min Nuri Sulṭānika, Wa'unsan Wa Farajan Min Baḥri Karamika, Anta Bīydika Al Amru Kullahu Wa-Maqālīda Kulah Shaī'in, Fahab Lanā Mā Taqurru Bihi 'Āyunnunā, Wa-Tughnīna 'An Sū'āli Ghairīka, Fā'innaka Was'iu Al-Karami, Kathīru Al-Jūdi, Ḥassanu'l Ashīami, Fī-Bābika Wāqifun, Wali-Jūdika Al-Wasi'ū Al-Ma'arufu Muntaẓirūn, Ya Karīm Ya Raḥīm.

Translation:

O Allah, the Lord of great mercy, O You who are aware of our secrets, our conscience, our obsessions, and our thoughts! Nothing escapes You.

I ask You for an abundant flow of Your goodness, a handful of the splendor of Your authority, and the comfort and relief of the ocean of Your generosity. You hold in your hand all power and the reins of all things.

Grant us that which is pleasing to our eyes and spare us the questions of others, for You are the Generous, the Free and the Benevolent. We are at your door, and we await your widespread and well-known generosity, O Generous and Most Merciful.

Source: At-Tirmidhī

Emergency Assistance

يا ودود يا ودود، يا ذا العرش المجيد، يا مبدئ يا معيد، يا فعالا لما يريد، أسألك بنور وجهك الذي ملأ أركان عرشك، وأسألك بقدرتك التي قدرت بها على جميع خلقك، وأسألك برحمتك التي وسعت كل شيء، لا إله إلا أنت، يا مغيث أغثني.

Transliteration:

Yā wadūd yā wadūd, yā dhal-'Arshi al-madjīd, yā mubdi'ū yā mu'īd, yā fa'ālan limā Yurīd, as-Allūka binuri wa-jahika al-ladhī mala'ā arkāna 'Arshika, wa as-Alūka bi-Qudratika al-latī Qadarta bihā 'ala Jamī'i Khalqika, wa as 'Allūka bi Raḥmatika alatī wass'iat kulla shaī', lā ilaha illā anta, yā mughīthu aghithnī.

Translation:

O You who fill us with affection. O You who fill us with affection. O You the Master of the Throne the All-Glorious. O You who certainly begins (the creation) and remakes it. O You who perfectly realizes what He wants.

I ask You by the light of Your Face that filled the pillars of Your Throne. And I ask You by Your Power through which Your Power is manifested over all Your creatures. And I ask You by Your Mercy which embraces all things. There is no other God but You. O You the Helper, come to my aid.

Source: Al-Ṭabarānī

Confidence in God (Tawakkul)

اللَّهُمَّ لَكَ الْحَمْدُ أَنْتَ قَيِّمُ السَّمَوَاتِ وَالأَرْضِ وَمَنْ فِيهِنَّ وَلَكَ الْحَمْدُ، لَكَ مُلْكُ السَّمَوَاتِ وَالأَرْضِ وَمَنْ فِيهِنَّ، وَلَكَ الْحَمْدُ أَنْتَ نُورُ السَّمَوَاتِ وَالأَرْضِ، وَلَكَ الْحَمْدُ أَنْتَ الْحَقُّ، وَوَعْدُكَ الْحَقُّ، وَلِقَاؤُكَ حَقٌّ، وَقَوْلُكَ حَقٌّ، وَالْجَنَّةُ حَقٌّ، وَالنَّارُ حَقٌّ، وَالنَّبِيُّونَ حَقٌّ، وَمُحَمَّدٌ ﷺ حَقٌّ، وَالسَّاعَةُ حَقٌّ، اللَّهُمَّ لَكَ أَسْلَمْتُ، وَبِكَ آمَنْتُ وَعَلَيْكَ تَوَكَّلْتُ، وَإِلَيْكَ أَنَبْتُ، وَبِكَ خَاصَمْتُ، وَإِلَيْكَ حَاكَمْتُ، فَاغْفِرْ لِي مَا قَدَّمْتُ وَمَا أَخَّرْتُ، وَمَا أَسْرَرْتُ وَمَا أَعْلَنْتُ، أَنْتَ الْمُقَدِّمُ وَأَنْتَ الْمُؤَخِّرُ، لَا إِلَهَ إِلاَّ أَنْتَ، وَلاَ حَوْلَ وَلاَ قُوَّةَ إِلاَّ بِاللَّهِ .

Transliteration:

Allāhumma laka al-Ḥamdu anta Qaiyum as-sammāwāti wal-arḍhi wa man fī-hinn. Wa-lakal-Ḥamdu laka mūlkus-samāwāti wal-arḍhi wa mann fī-hinna. Wa-lakal-Ḥamdu anta nurus-samāwāti wal-arḍi. Wa-lakal-Ḥamdu anta-al-Ḥaqqu wa-wa-'duka-al-Ḥaqqu, wa-liqā'uka Ḥaqun, wa-Qauwluka Ḥaqun, wal-Jannatu Ḥaqun wan-nāru Ḥaqqun wan-nabīyūna Ḥaqqun Wa Muḥammadan, Ṣallal-lahu'alaīhi wasallama, Ḥaqqun, was-sā'atu Ḥaqqun. Allāhumma laka aslamtu wa-bika Āmantu, wa 'alaīyka Tawwakaltu, wa-ilaīyka Anabtu wa-bika Khāṣamtu, wa-ilaīyka Ḥakamtu faghfir lī mā Qaddamtu wa mā akhartu wa mā as-rartu wa mā a'lantu, 'anta al-Muqaddimu wa anta al-mu'akhiru, lā ilaha illā anta, wa lā Ḥaula wa lā Quwata illā Billāh.

Translation:

O Allah! All the praises are for you. You hold the Heavens and the Earth, and whatever is in them. To You is all praise. You have the possession of the Heavens and the Earth and whatever is in them. All praise is to You. You are the Light of the heavens and the earth. All the praises are for You.

You are the truth, Your promise is the truth, and meeting You is true. Your word is truth, heaven is truth, hell is truth, and all the prophets (peace be upon them) are truth. And Muhammad, peace and blessing of God upon him (ﷺ), is true, and the day of resurrection is true.

O Allah! I entrust myself to You. I believe in You and rely on You. And I repent to You. By You, I fight (Your enemies) and by Your law I judge. Forgive me, my past and future sins, those committed in secret and those committed in public. You are the one who makes things go forward and backward, no other god but You. There is no strength and power except in You.

Source: al-Bukhārī (1120)

Praise and Forgiveness

اللهم لك أسلمت، وبك آمنت، وعليك توكلت، وبك خاصمت وإليك حاكمت، فاغفر لى ما قدمت وما أخرت، وما أسررت وما أعلنت، أنت المقدم وأنت المؤخر. لا إله إلا أنت. أنت الأول والأخر والظاهر والباطن، عليك توكلت، وأنت رب العرش العظيم.

Transliteration:

Allāhumma laka aslamtu, wa-bika Āmintu, wa‘alīyka Tawakaltu, wa-bika Khāṣamtu wa ilīyka Ḥakamtu, faghfir lī mā Qadamtu wa mā Akhartu, wa mā Asrartu wa mā ‘Ālantu, anta al-Muqadimu wa anta al-Muakhiru. Lā ilaha illā anta. Anta al-Awalu wa'l-Akhiru wal-Ẓahiru wal-Baṭinu, ‘alīyka Tawakaltu, wa anta Rabbi al-Arshi al-Aẓīm.

Translation:

O Allah! I trust in You. I believe in You and I rely on You. And I repent to You. In You have I put my trust. By You have I fought (Your enemies), and by Your Law have I judged.

So forgive me my past and future sins, those committed in secret and those committed in public.

There is no other God but You, the First and the Last, the External and the Internal. In You, I place my trust, for You are the Lord of the Supreme Throne.

Source: Ṣaḥiḥ Muslim 769

Repentance and Spiritual Purification

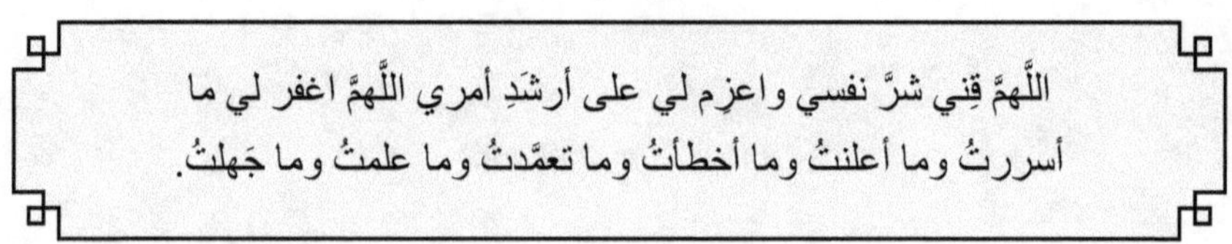

Transliteration:

Allāhumma Qinī Sharra Nafsī Wa-'Azim lī 'Ala Ārshadi Amrī Allāhumma Ighfirlī Mā Asrartu Wa mā 'Āllantu Wa mā Akhṭ'atu Wa mā Ta'mmadtu Wa mā 'Alimtu Wa mā Jahiltu.

Translation:

O Allah, protect me from the evil in me and guide me in my actions. O Allah, forgive me for what I have hidden, what I have said, what I have done wrong, what I have done intentionally, what I knew and what I did not know.

Source: ibn Al Qayyīm al-Jawzīyah

Protection Against the False Messiah

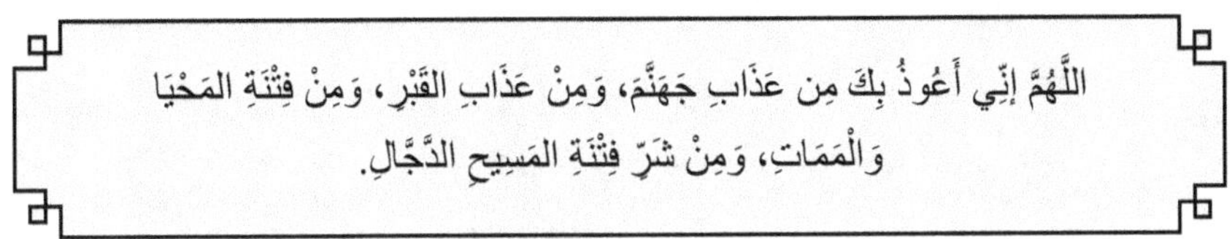

Transliteration:

Allāhumma inni A'ūzu Bika Min 'Azābi Jahannam, Wa Min 'Azābil-Qabr, Wa Min Fitnatil-Maḥyā Wal-Mamāt, Wa Min Syarri Fitnatil-Masīḥil-Dajjāl.

Translation:

O Allah, I seek refuge with You against the torment of Hell, against the torments of the grave, against the temptations of life and death and against the evil of the temptation of the Antichrist.

Source: Ṣaḥiḥ Muslim

Mercy in this World and the Hereafter

اللهمَّ مالكَ الملكِ تُؤتي الملكَ مَن تشاءُ، وتنزعُ الملكَ ممن تشاءُ، وتُعِزُّ مَن تشاءُ، وتذِلُّ مَن تشاءُ، بيدِك الخيرُ إنك على كلِّ شيءٍ قديرٌ. رحمنُ الدنيا والآخرةِ ورحيمُهما، تعطيهما من تشاءُ، وتمنعُ منهما من تشاءُ، ارحمْني برحمتك.

Transliteration:

Allāhumma Mālik al-Mūlki Tu'tī al-Mūlka Man Tashā'u, Wa-Tanzi'u al-Mūlka Mim-Man Tashā'u, Wa-Tu'izu Man Tashā'u, Wa-Tūdhilu Man Tashā'u, Bīydika Al-Khaīyru innaka 'Ala Kulli Shīy'in Qadīhrun. Raḥman Ad-Dunīya Wal-Ākhīrati Wa-Raḥīmu-huma, Tuṭīhima Man Tashā'u, Wa-Tamna'u Min-Huma Man Tashā'u, Arḥamnī Bi-Raḥmatika.

Translation:

O Allah, You are the King of the universe. You give power to whom You will, and You take it from whom You will. You honor whom You will, and You humble whom You will. In Your hand is all good, and You are above all things. O Merciful One of this world and the hereafter, have mercy on me with Your mercy.

Source: Al-Albānī, in Ṣaḥīḥ Anas ibn Mālik

Protection Against Dictators and Oppressors

اللَّهمَّ ربَّ السَّمواتِ السَّبعِ وربَّ العرشِ العظيمِ كن لي جارًا من فلانِ بنِ فلانٍ وأحزابِهِ من خلائقِكَ أن يفرطَ عليَّ أحدٌ منْهم أو يَطغى عزَّ جارُكَ وجلَّ ثناؤُكَ و لا إلَهَ إلَّا أنتَ

Transliteration:

Allāhumma Rabba As-samāwāti As-sab'ī, Wa Rabba al-'Arshi'l 'Aẓīmi, Kun Lī Jāran Min [Fulān Bin Fulān], Wa Aḥz-bihi Min Khalā'iqika, An Yafruṭa 'Alaīyya Aḥadun Minhum Awu Yaṭgha' 'Aza Jārūka, Wa-Jalla Thanā'uka, Wa Lā Ilaha Illā Anta.

Translation:

O Allah, Lord of the seven heavens, Lord of the exalted throne! Grant me Your assistance against ('this one and that one') and his helpers among Your creatures, so that not one of them treats me badly or wrongs me. Mighty is Your protection, and glorious are Your praises. There is no God but You.

Source: Sahih Al Albānī 545

Drought (Rain)

اللهم اسقنا غيثاً مغيثاً مريئاً نافعاً غير ضار، اللهم اسقنا غيثاً مغيثاً مريئاً نافعاً غير ضار، اللهم أنت الله لا إله إلا أنت، أنت الغنى ونحن الفقراء، أنزل علينا الغيث، واجعل ما أنزلت لنا قوة وبلاغاً إلى حين، اللهم إنّا نسألك خيرها وخير ما فيها، وخير ما أرسلت به، ونعوذ بك من شرها، وشر ما فيها، وشر ما أرسلت به، اللهم لا تقتلنا بغضبك، ولا تهلكنا بعذابك، سبحان الذي يسبح الرعد والملائكة بحمده.

Transliteration:

Allāhumma Asqinā Ghīythann Mughīthann Marī'ann Nāfi'an Ghaīyra Ḍārin, Allāhumma Asqina Ghīythann Mughīthann Marī'ann Nāfi'an Ghaīyra Ḍārin. Allāhumma Anta Allāhu Lā Illaha Illā Anta, Anta Al-Ghanīhu Wa-naḥnu Al-Fuqarā', Anzil 'Alīyna Al-Ghīytha, Wa-J'al Mā Anzalta Lanā Quwatan Wa-Balāghan Ila Ḥīna. Allāhumma innā Nas'alūka Khaīyraha Wa-Khaīyra Mā Fīha, Wa-Khaīyra Mā Ursilat Bihi, Wa-na'ūdu Bika Min Sharriha, Wa-sharri Mā Fīhā, Wa-Sharri Ma Ursilat Bihi. Allāhumma La Taqtūlnā Bi-Ghadabika, Wa lā Tūhlikanā Bi-'Adhābika, Subḥāna Al-ladhī Yusabbiḥu Al-R'adu Wal-Mala'iykatu Bi-Ḥamdihi.

Translation:

O Allah, grant us beneficial, useful, fertile, profitable and safe rain. O Allah, grant us the relief of abundant, beneficial and safe rain.

O Allah, You are the Lord. There is no other God but You. You are the Richest and we are the poor. Send down upon us the saving rain, and make of what You have sent down a power that will enables us to live for a time.

O Allah, we ask You for its goodness, the goodness of what it contains, and the goodness that it brings with it. And we seek refuge in You from the harm, inconvenience, and all the evil that the rain may bring.

O Allah, do not kill us with Your anger and do not destroy us with Your punishment. Praise be to Allah, the thunder and the angels celebrate His glory and praise.

Source: Al-Bukhārī

Great Misery and Distress

يا مقيل العثرات يا قاضي الحاجات اقضِ حاجتي وفرّج كربتي
وارزقني من حيث لا أحتسب، إلهي أدعوك دعاء مَن اشتدّت فاقته
وضعفت قوّته وقلّت حيلته دعاء الغريق المضطر البائس الفقير الذي
لا يجد لكشف ما هو فيه مِن الذنوب إلا أنت، واكشف ما بي مِن ضرّ،
إنك أرحم الراحمين لا إله إلا أنتَ سبحانك إنّي كنت من الظالمين،
سبحان الله وبحمده عدد خلقه، ورضا نفسه، وزنة عرشه ومداد كلماته.

Transliteration:

Yā Muqīla Al-'Atharāti Ya Qāḍīya al-Ḥajātī aqḍi Ḥajātī Wa-Farrij
Karbatī Wa-Arzūqnī Min Ḥaīythu Lā Aḥtasibu, Īlahī 'Addūka Du'ā Man
Ishtaddat Fāqatuhu Wa-ḍa'ūfat Quwwatahu Wa Qallat Ḥilatuhu, Dú'ā Al-
Gharīqi Al-Muḍṭari Al-bā'isu Al-faqīru Al-ladhī Lā Yajidu Lī-Kashfi Mā
Hua Fīhi Min Al-dhūnubi Illa Anta, Wakshif Mā Bī Min Ḍarrin, Innaka
Ar-ḥamu Ar-Rahimīna Lā Ilaha Illā Anta Subḥānaka Innī Kūntu Mina
Al-Ẓalimīna, Subḥāna Allāh Wa-bi-ḥamdihi 'Adada Khalqihi, Wariḍa
Nafsihi, Wa-zinata 'Arshihi Wa-Midāda Kalimātihi.

Translation:

O Lord! O You who remove the stumbling blocks and ease the difficulties, O Reliever of distress! Help me in my distress, ease my fear and provide me with everything I need, even that which I do not expect.

O Allah, I ask You to grant my request, for my distress is great, my strength is weak, and my abilities are reduced. I implore You as a drowning, afflicted, miserable, poor person who invokes You and who has no way to relieve his sins except from You.

O Allah! Deliver me from my suffering, for You are the Most Merciful of the Merciful. There is no other God but You. Glory be to You! I was among the unjust. Honor, purity and praise to Allah, as many times as the universe counts His creations to be satisfied. As many times as they resemble the weight of His throne and the indefinite number of His words.

Source: Muslim

Life Without Worries

اللهم يا مؤنسي في وحدتي، ويا راحمي في غربتي، ويا وليّ نعمتي،
ويا مفرّج كربتي، ويا سامع دعوتي، ويا مُقيل عثرتي، ويا راحم
دمعتي، يا رجائي في الضيق، ويا رب البيت العتيق، ارزقني من
عندك رزقاً واسعاً طيبا مباركا فيه.

اللهُمّ إني أعوذُ بكَ منَ الهمِّ والحزَنِ، وأعوذُ بكَ منَ العجز والكسلِ،
وأعوذُ بكَ منَ الجُبنِ والبخلِ، وأعوذُ بكَ مِن غلبةِ الدَّينِ وقهرِ الرجالِ.

Transliteration:

Allāhumma yā mu'nisī fī waḥdatī, wa yā rāḥimī fī Ghurbatī, wa yā walī' ni'matī, wa yā Mufarija Kurbatī, Wa yā Sāmi'a 'Dawatī, Wa yā Mūqīla 'Athratī, Wa yā Rāḥima Damm'atī Yā Rajā'ī Fī-Ḍīqi, Wa yā Rabba al-Baīt Al-'Atīqi, Arzūqnī Min 'indika Rizqan Wasi'an Ṭaīyban Mubārakan Fīhi. Allāhumma innī A'ūdhu Bika Min Al-Hammi Wal-Ḥuzni, Wa a'ūdhu Bika Min Al-Ajzi Wal-Kassali, Wa a'ūdhu Bika Min Al-Jūbni Wal-Būkhli, Wa a'ūdhu Bika Min Ghalabati Al-Dīni Wa Qahari Ar-Rijāli.

Translation:

O Allah, the Comforter in my loneliness, the Merciful in my alienation, the Guardian of my bliss, the Reliever in my affliction, the Hearer of my supplications, the Merciful in my tears, the Hope in my despair, and the

Lord of the House of Allah! Grant me from Your Kingdom abundant, good and blessed sustenance.

O Allah, I seek refuge in You from anxiety and sorrow. I seek refuge in You from incapacity and laziness. I seek refuge with You against cowardice, greed, and the difficulty of debt and the oppression of men.

Source: Ṣaḥiḥ Al Bukhārī

Reaching Paradise

اللهُمَّ إِنِّي أَسْأَلُكَ مِنَ الْخَيْرِ كُلِّهِ عَاجِلِهِ وَآجِلِهِ، مَا عَلِمْتُ مِنْهُ وَمَا لَمْ

أَعْلَمْ، وَأَعُوذُ بِكَ مِنَ الشَّرِّ كُلِّهِ، عَاجِلِهِ وَأَجِلِهِ مَا عَلِمْتُ مِنْهُ، وَمَا لَمْ

أَعْلَمْ، اللهُمَّ إِنِّي أَسْأَلُكَ مِنْ خَيْرِ مَا سَأَلَكَ عَبْدُكَ وَنَبِيُّكَ مُحَمَّدٌ صَلَّى اللهُ

عَلَيْهِ وَسَلَّمَ ، وَأَعُوذُ بِكَ مِنْ شَرِّ مَا عَاذَ مِنْهُ عَبْدُكَ وَنَبِيُّكَ مُحَمَّدٌ صَلَّى

اللهُ عَلَيْهِ وَسَلَّمَ، اللهُمَّ إِنِّي أَسْأَلُكَ الْجَنَّةَ وَمَا قَرَّبَ إِلَيْهَا مِنْ قَوْلٍ أَوْ عَمَلٍ،

وَأَعُوذُ بِكَ مِنَ النَّارِ وَمَا قَرَّبَ إِلَيْهَا مِنْ قَوْلٍ أَوْ عَمَلٍ ، وَأَسْأَلُكَ أَنْ تَجْعَلَ

كُلَّ قَضَاءٍ تَقْضِيهِ لِي خَيْرًا.

Transliteration:

Allāhumma innī as'Allūka min al-khaīyri Kullihi 'Ājilihi Wa-Ājilihi, Mā 'Alimtu Minhu Wa mā Lam 'Ālam, Wa a'ūdhu Bika Mina Al-Shari Kulihi, 'Ājilihi Wa-Ājilihi Mā 'Alimtu Minhu, Wa mā Lam 'Ālam, Allāhumma innī as-alūkka Min Khaīyri Mā Sā'alaka 'Abduka Wa-Nabīyuka Muḥamadun Ṣallal-lahu'alaīhi wa-sallama, Wa a'ūdhu Bika Min Shari Ma 'Āadha Minhu 'Abduka Wa-Nabīyuka Muḥamadun Ṣallal-lahu'alaīhi wasallama, Allāhumma innī As'aluka Al-Jannata Wa mā Qaraba Ilīyha Min Qawlin Auw 'Amalin, Wa a'ūdhu Bika Mina Al-Nāri Wa mā Qaraba Ilīyha Min Qawlin Auw 'Amalin, Wa as'aluka An Ta'jala Kulla Qaḍa'in Taqḍihi Lī Khaīyran.

Translation:

O Allah, I ask You for all goodness in the present and the future, what I know and what I do not know. O Allah, I seek refuge with You from all evil, in the present and the future, what I know and what I do not know.

O Allah, I ask You for the good that Your slave and Prophet has asked You for, and I seek refuge with You from the evil from which Your slave and Prophet sought refuge.

O Allah, I ask You for Paradise and for that which brings one closer to is, in word and deed, and I seek refuge in You from Hell and from that which brings one closer to is, in word and deed.

And I ask You to make every decree that You decree concerning me good.

Source: Al Albānī 1276, Sunan ibn Mājah 3846

Istikhara Du'ā for Decisions

اللهُمَّ إِنِّي أَسْتَخِيرُكَ بِعِلْمِكَ، وَأَسْتَقْدِرُكَ بِقُدْرَتِكَ، وَأَسْأَلُكَ مِنْ فَضْلِكَ العَظِيمِ، فَإِنَّكَ تَقْدِرُ وَلا أَقْدِرُ، وَتَعْلَمُ وَلا أَعْلَمُ، وَأَنْتَ عَلاَّمُ الغُيُوبِ، اللهُمَّ إِنْ كُنْتَ تَعْلَمُ أن هذا الأمرَ ـ وَيُسمِّي حَاجَتَه ـ خَيرٌ لِي في دِيني وَمَعَاشي وَعَاقِبَةِ أَمْري ـ أوْ قالَ: عَاجِلِهِ وآجِلِهِ ـ فاقْدُرْهُ لِي وَيَسِّرْهُ لِي، ثُمَّ بَارِكْ لِي فِيهِ، وإِنْ كُنْتَ تَعْلَمُ أنَّ هذا الأمرَ شَرٌّ لِي في دِيني وَمَعَاشي وَعَاقِبَةِ أمري ـ أوْ قالَ: عَاجِلِهِ وآجِلِهِ ـ فاصْرِفْهُ عَنِّي، وَاصْرِفْنِي عَنْهُ، واقْدُرْ لِيَ الخَيْرَ حَيْثُ كَانَ، ثُمَّ أرْضِنِي بِهِ.

Transliteration:

Allāhumma innī Astakhīrukaq Bi-'ilmika Wa-Astaqdiruka Bi-Qudratika Wa As-alūka Min Faḍlika'l 'Aẓīmi, Fā-innaka Taqdiru Wa lā Aqdiru Wa T'alamu Wa lā 'Ālamu Wa Anta 'Allām al-Ghuyūbi. Allāhumma in Kunta T'alamu Anna Hadhal Amra--w-Yūsamī Ḥājatuhu--Khaīyrun Lī Fī Dīnī Wa Mā-shī Wa 'Āqibatī Amrī- 'Aw Qāl: Ājilihi Wa-Ājilihi- Faqdirhu Lī Wa Yassirhu Lī, Thumma Barik Lī Fīhi, Wa in Kunta T'alamu Anna Hadhal Amra Sharrun Lī Fī Dīnī Wa Ma'āshi Wa 'Āqibati Amrī- 'Aw Qāl: Ājilihi Wa-Ājilihi- Faṣrifhu 'Annī Wa-ṣrifnī 'Anhu, Waqdir Lī'l al-Khaīyra Ḥaīthu Kāna, Thumma Arḍinī Bihi.

Translation:

O Allah, I seek the counsel of Your Knowledge, and I seek the help of Your Omnipotence, and I beseech You for Your Magnificent Grace. Surely, You are Capable and I am not. You know, and I do not know, and You are the Knower of the unseen.

O Allah, if You know that this matter ['the thing to be decided'] is good for me in my religion and in my life and for my welfare in the life to come, then order it for me and make it easy for me, then bless me in it.

And if You know that this matter is bad for me in my religion and in my life and for my welfare in the life to come, then take it away from me, and take me away from it. And order me the good wherever it may be. And help me to be satisfied with it.

Source: Al Bukhārī 7/162

Protection against Evil People and Earthly Spirits (Jinns)

اللهُ أكبرُ، اللهُ أعزُّ من خلقِه جميعًا، اللهُ أعزُّ مما أخافُ وأحذرُ، وأعوذُ بالله الذي لا إله إلا هو، الممسكُ السماواتِ السبعَ أن يقعنَ على الأرضِ إلا بإذنِه؛ من شرّ عبدِك فلانٍ، وجنودِه وأتباعِه وأشياعِه، من الجنّ والإنسِ، اللهمَّ كن لي جارًا من شرّهم، جلَّ ثناؤُك، وعزَّ جارُك، وتباركَ اسمُك ولا إله غيرُك.

Transliteration:

Allāhu Akbaru, Allāhu 'āzu min khalqihi Jamī'an, Allāhu ' 'āzu mimmā akhāfu wa-Aḥdharu, wa-a'ūthu billāhi al-ladhī lā ilaha illā hua, al-mummsiku as-sammāwāti as-sab'i an yaqa'na 'ala'l arḍhi illā bi-idhnihi, min sharri 'abdika [fulān], wa-Junudihi wa-Atbā'ihi wa-Ashīyā'ihi, min al-Jinn wa'l insi, Allāhumma kun lī Jaran min sharrihim, Jalla Thana'ūka wa-'āza Jarūka, wa-Tabaraka is-mūka, wa lā illa ha Ghaīyruka.

Translation:

Allah is the Almighty, and He is more powerful than all His creation. He is also more powerful than what I fear and what I abhor. I seek refuge in Allah, for none is worthy of worship except Him.

On Whom depends the collapse of the heavens upon the earth, against the evil of such a one (name him), his allies and followers, Jinn or human.

I seek refuge in You, O Allah, against the evil of Your servant [name of the person] and his allies and followers, among the jinn and humans. O Allah, be my protector against their evil. Glorious are Your praises, and mighty is Your protection. Blessed be Your name! There is no true God but You!

Source: Sahih Al Albānī 546

Overcome Fears and Protection

بسم اللهِ خيرِ الأسماءِ في الأرضِ وفي السماءِ، بسمِ الله أفتتحُ وبه أختتم، اللهُ ربِّي لا أشركُ به شيئاً، اللهُ أكبرُ، اللهُ أكبرُ، اللهُ أعزُّ من خلقِه جميعًا، اللهُ أعزُّ مما أخافُ وأحذرُ، بكَ اللهمَّ أعوذُ من شرِّ نفسي، ومن شرِّ غيري، ومن شرِّ ما خلقَ ربِّي وذرأَ وبرأَ، وبكَ اللهمَّ أحترزُ منهم، وبكَ اللهمَّ أعوذُ بكَ من شرورهم، وبكَ اللهمَّ أدرأُ في نحورهم.

Transliteration:

Bismillahi khaīyri'l asamā'i fī'l arḍi wa fī as-samā'i, bismillahi 'aftatiḥu wa bihi akhtatimu, Allāhu Rabbī lā ushriku bihi sha'ī-an, Allāhu Akhbaru, Allāhu Akhbaru, Allahu Akhbaru, Allāhu 'Āzu min khalqihi Jamī'an, Allāhu 'Āzu mimmā Akhāfu wa Aḥdharu, bika Allāhumma a'ūdhu min sharri nafsī, wamin sharri ghayrī, wamin sharri mā khalaqa rabbī wadhara'a wabarra'a, wa bika Allāhumma aḥtarrizu minhum wa bika Allāhumma a'ūdhu bika min shururihim wa bika Allāhumma 'adarra'u fī nurḥurihim.

Translation:

In the name of Allah, the best of all names on earth and in heaven! In the name of Allah I begin and with Him I end. Allah is my Lord, nothing do I associate with Him. Allah is great, Allah is great, Allah is great.

Allah is more important than all His creation. Allah is stronger than all that I fear and am afraid of.

In You, O Allah, I seek refuge from the evil within myself, from the evil of others, and from the evil that my Lord has created, brought forth, and nurtured.

By You, O Allah, I take refuge from it. In You, O Allah, I seek refuge from their evils, and in You, O Allah, I turn away from them.

Source: Imām Al-Nawawī

Praise and Tawhīd

اللّهم خذ بيدي إلى الهداية واستر عليّ وعلى جميع المسلمين. الحمد لله، الحمد لله، الحمد لله، الحمد لله حمداً كثيراً طيباً مباركاً كما ينبغي لجلال وجهه وعظيم سلطانه، وصلّ اللهم على محمد وعلى آله وصحبه أجمعين. لا إله إلّا الله الملك الحق، لا إله إلّا الله الملك الحق المبين، لا إله إلّا الله العدل اليقين، لا إله إلّا الله ربنا ورب آبائنا الأولين، سبحانك إنّي كنت من الظالمين، لا إله إلّا الله وحده لا شريك له له الملك وله الحمد يحيي ويميت وهو حيٌّ لا يموت، بيده الخير وإليه المصير وهو على كل شيء قدير. لا إله إلّا الله إقراراً بربوبيته، سبحان الله خضوعاً لعظمته.

Transliteration:

Allāhumma khudh bīyadī 'ila'l hidāyati wa-stur 'alaya wa 'ala Jamī'i al-Muslimīna. Al-Ḥamdulillāhi, Al-Ḥamdulillāhi, Al-Ḥamdulillāhi, Al-Ḥamdulillāhi, Al-Ḥamdulillāhi, Ḥamdan kathīyran Ṭayīban mubarākan kamā yanbaghī li Jalāli wa-Jahihi wa-'aẓīmi Sulṭānihi, wa-Ṣalli Allāhumma 'ala Muḥammad wa 'ala Ālihi wa-Ṣaḥbihi Ajma'īn, lā 'ilaha 'illā Allāh al-Māliku al-Ḥaqqu, lā ilaha illā Allāh al-Māliku al-Ḥaqu al-Mūbīn, lā ilaha illā Allāh al-'adlul al- yaqīn, lā ilaha illā Allāh rabanā wa-Rabu Ābāīyina al-Awalīna, subḥānaka innī kuntu mina aẓ-ẓālimīna, lā ilaha illā Allāh wa-Ḥadahu lā sharīka lahu, lahu al-mūlku wa-lahu al-Ḥamdu yūḥyī wa-yūmit wa-hua Ḥayun lā yamūt, bīydihi al-khaīyru wa 'ilaīyhi al-maṣīr wa-hua 'ala kulli shaī'in Qadīr. lā ilaha illā Allāh iqrāran bi-Rububīytihi, Subbḥān Allāh khuḍhu'an li-aẓamatihi.

Translation:

Oh, Allah, take my hand, guide me and protect me - and all Muslims. Praise be to God, praise be to God, praise be to God, praise be to God!

Thanks be to Him, O Benevolent and Glorified One, according to the glory of His countenance and the Greatness of His power. Blessings and peace be upon Muhammad (ﷺ), his family and all his companions.

There is no god but Allah, the true King. There is no God except Allah, the manifest truth.

There is no God except Allah, the Righteous and the Constant. There is no God except Allah, our Lord, and the Lord of our ancestors.

There is no God but Allah alone, Who has no partner. To Him belongs the kingdom, and to Him belongs all praise. He gives life and death, and He is living who does not die.

To Him belongs all good, and to Him belongs the lot. He has power over all things. There is no God but Allah, in recognition of His glory. Glory be to Allah in recognition of His strength.

Source: Ṣaḥiḥ Muslim

Guide on the Right Path

اللَّهُمَّ ارْحَمْنِي بِتَرْكِ الْمَعَاصِي أَبَدًا مَا أَبْقَيْتَنِي وَارْحَمْنِي أَنْ أَتَكَلَّفَ مَا لاَ يَعْنِينِي وَارْزُقْنِي حُسْنَ النَّظَرِ فِيمَا يُرْضِيكَ عَنِّي اللَّهُمَّ بَدِيعَ السَّمَوَاتِ وَالأَرْضِ ذَا الْجَلاَلِ وَالإِكْرَامِ وَالْعِزَّةِ الَّتِي لاَ تُرَامُ أَسْأَلُكَ يَا اللهُ يَا رَحْمَنُ بِجَلاَلِكَ وَنُورِ وَجْهِكَ أَنْ تُلْزِمَ قَلْبِي حِفْظَ كِتَابِكَ كَمَا عَلَّمْتَنِي وَارْزُقْنِي أَنْ أَتْلُوَهُ عَلَى النَّحْوِ الَّذِي يُرْضِيكَ عَنِّي اللَّهُمَّ بَدِيعَ السَّمَوَاتِ وَالأَرْضِ ذَا الْجَلاَلِ وَالإِكْرَامِ وَالْعِزَّةِ الَّتِي لاَ تُرَامُ أَسْأَلُكَ يَا اللهُ يَا رَحْمَنُ بِجَلاَلِكَ وَنُورِ وَجْهِكَ أَنْ تُنَوِّرَ بِكِتَابِكَ بَصَرِي وَأَنْ تُطْلِقَ بِهِ لِسَانِي وَأَنْ تُفَرِّجَ بِهِ عَنْ قَلْبِي وَأَنْ تَشْرَحَ بِهِ صَدْرِي وَأَنْ تَغْسِلَ بِهِ بَدَنِي لأَنَّهُ لاَ يُعِينُنِي عَلَى الْحَقِّ غَيْرُكَ وَلاَ يُؤْتِيهِ إِلاَّ أَنْتَ وَلاَ حَوْلَ وَلاَ قُوَّةَ إِلاَّ بِاللهِ الْعَلِيِّ الْعَظِيمِ.

Transliteration:

Allāhumma ar-Ḥamnī bi-tarkil-ma'āṣī abadan mā abqaīytanī, wa-arḥamnī an ata-kallafa mā lā ya'nīnī, warzūqnī ḥusnan-naẓari fī mā yurḍīka 'annī. Allāhumma badī'as-samāwāti wal-arḍi dhal-Jalāli wal-ikrāmi wal-'izatil-latī lā tūrāmu, as'Aluka yā Allāhu yā Raḥmānu bi-Jalālika wa nūri wa-Jhika, an tulzima Qalbī Ḥifẓa kitābika kamā 'allamtanī, wa-razuqnī an at-luwahu 'alan-naḥwi aladhī yurḍīka 'annī Allāhumma badī'as-samāwāti wal-arḍi dhal-Jalāli wal-ikrāmi wal 'izatillatī lā tūrāmu, as'Aluka yā Allāhu yā Raḥmānu bi-Jalālika wa nūri wa-Jhika, an tunauwirabi-kitābika baṣṣarī, wa an tuṭliqa bihi lisānī, wa an tufarrija bihi 'an Qalbī, wa an tashraḥa bihi ṣadrī, wa an taghsila bihi badanī, li-annahu lā yu'īnunī 'ala al-Ḥaqqi ghaīyruka wa lā yu'tīhi illā anta wa lā ḥaula wa lā quwwata illā billāhil 'Alīyyil 'Aẓīmi.

Translation:

O Allah, have mercy on me by keeping me from sins as long as you keep me alive. And have mercy on me by not taking upon me that which does not concern me Show me that which satisfies You with me. O Allah, Creator of the heavens and the earth, Lord of glory, bounty and unsurpassed honor. I ask You, O Allah, O Merciful One, by Your glory and the light of Your face, to command my heart to learn Your Book, as You have taught it to me, and to recite it in such a way as to please You.

O Allah, Creator of the heavens and the earth, Lord of glory, wealth and unsurpassed honor! I beseech You, O Allah, O Most Gracious, by Your glory and the light of Your face, to enlighten my eyesight with the Holy Qur'an, to free my tongue from it, to enlighten my heart from it, to expand my chest from it, and to wash my body from it. No one but You helps me to reach the truth, and no one but You imparts it. There is no power and no strength except with Allah, the Most High, the Magnificent.

Source: at-Tirmidhī

Purification of the Soul

اللَّهُمَّ إِنِّي أَعُوذُ بِكَ مِنَ الْعَجْزِ وَالْكَسَلِ وَالْجُبْنِ وَالْبُخْلِ وَالْهَرَمِ وَعَذَابِ الْقَبْرِ اللَّهُمَّ آتِ نَفْسِي تَقْوَاهَا وَزَكِّهَا أَنْتَ خَيْرُ مَنْ زَكَّاهَا أَنْتَ وَلِيُّهَا وَمَوْلَاهَا اللَّهُمَّ إِنِّي أَعُوذُ بِكَ مِنْ عِلْمٍ لَا يَنْفَعُ وَمِنْ قَلْبٍ لَا يَخْشَعُ وَمِنْ نَفْسٍ لَا تَشْبَعُ وَمِنْ دَعْوَةٍ لَا يُسْتَجَابُ لَهَا.

Transliteration:

Allāhumma innī aʿūdhu bika min alʿazji wal-kassali wal-Jubni wal-Bukhli wal-Harami wa ʿadhābi al-Qabri Allāhumma Āti nafsī taqwāha wazakkāhā anta khaīyru man zakkāhā anta walīuhā wa-maulāhā Allāhumma innī aʿūdhu bika min ʿilmin lā yanfaʿu wa-min Qalbin lā yakhshaʿu wa min nafsin lā tashbaʿu wa min daʿwatin lā yustajābu lahā.

Translation:

O Allah, I seek refuge in You from inability, from sloth, from cowardice, from avarice, from decrepitude, and from the torments of the grave. O Allah, give my soul the sense of righteousness and purify it, for You are its best Purifier. You are its protective friend and its guardian.

O Allah, I seek refuge in You from knowledge that is of no avail, from the heart that does not cherish fear, from the soul that does not feel satisfied, and from supplication that is not answered.

Source: Ṣaḥiḥ Muslim 2722

Ask with the Most Beautiful Names of Allah

اللهم إنا نسألُك باسمك الأعظم الطاهر المُطهر المبارك المكنون الذي إذا سُئلت به أعطيتنا وإذا دُعيت به أجبتنا وإذا استُرحمت به رحمتنا وإذا استفرجت به فرجت عنا. يا بر يا تواب يا رحمن يا رحيم يا فرد يا صمد يا الله يا من لم يلد ولم يولد ولم يكن له كفواً أحد. يا حنان يا منان يا حي يا قيوم يا من له الأسماء الحُسنى والصفات العلى نسألك صحة بلا علل وإيمانًا بلا خلل وعملاً بلا جدل، ونعوذ بك من غرور الأمل والخطأ والزلل وضعف البدن، وضيق السُبل.

Transliteration:

Allāhumma innā nas'aluka bi-ismika al-Āẓamu al-Ṭāhiru al-Muṭhaharu al-Mubārak al-Maknūn al-ladhī idhā sui'ylta bihi 'Āṭayītanā wa-idhā du'īyta bihi adjabtanā wa-idhā as-Turḥamta bihi Raḥamtana wa-idhā ustufrijta bihi farajata 'annā. Yā Barru ya Tawābu yā Raḥmanu yā Raḥim yā fardun yā Ṣamadu yā Allāh yā mann lam yalid wa-lam yūlad wa-lam yakun lahu kufu'an aḥadu. Yā Ḥanānu Yā Manānu Yā Ḥayu Yā Qayyūm yā man lahu al-Asmā'u al-Ḥusna wal-Ṣifātu 'alula. Nas'āluka Ṣiḥatan bilā 'elal wa-'iymānan bilā khalal wa-'amalan bila Jadall, wa na'ūdhu bika min ghururi al-amal wal-khaṭa'u wal-zūlal wa-ḍ'uf al-badani, wa-ḍīqi as-subūli.

Translation:

O Allah, I ask You in Your Great, Immaculate, Purified, Blessed and Hidden Name, through which, when one asks You, You give to us. And if You are called by it, You answer us And when one asks for forgiveness through him, You free us.

O Righteous, Merciful, Gracious, Compassionate, One and Only, Unshakable, O Allah, Who was not begotten, did not beget, and had no equal. O Merciful, O Generous, O Living, O Eternal, Who has the most beautiful names and highest attributes.

O God, to You we pray, and we prostrate, and to You we seek, we hope for Your mercy and fear Your punishment.

We ask You for health without blemish, for faith without doubt, and for deeds without (inner) resistance. We seek refuge in You from deceptive hope, error, aberration, physical weakness and difficulties.

Source: At-Ṭabarānī

Concerns and Issues

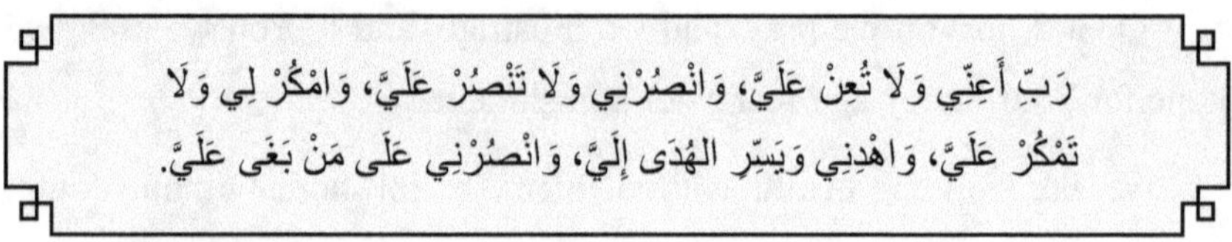

Transliteration:

Rabbi ‘Āinnī wa lā tu‘in ‘alayya, wan-Ṣurnī wa-lā tanṣur ‘alayya, wam-kūr-lī wa-lā tamkūr ‘alayya, wahdinī wa-yassiri al-Huda’ ilaīyya, wan-Ṣurnī ‘ala man Bagha ‘alayya.

Translation:

My Lord, help me and do not give help against me; grant me victory, and do not grant victory over me; plan on my behalf and do not plan against me; guide me, and made my right guidance easy for me; grant me victory over those who act wrongfully towards me.

Source: Sunan Abi Dawūd 1510

Unity and Protection of Muslims

اللهم اجعل القرآن العظيم زادنا وسندنا والسُنة المطهرة حبّنا ومددنا،
واحفظنا من تفرُق كلمتنا واعصمنا من شتات أمرنا ولا تجعلنا فِرقًا
وشيعاً، نُخالف بعضنا واجعل صلاتنا للبلاء واقية، وللأمراض شافية،
واجعل تلاوتنا للقرآن مُنجية، ومن النار كافية واجعل نفوسنا صافية
وفى الآخرة راضية، يا من لا تضيع عنده الودائع.

Transliteration:

Allāhumma aj'al al-Qur'ān al-'Aẓima Zādanā wa-sanadanā wa-sūnata al-Mūṭaharati Ḥubbanā wa-Madadanā, wa-Ḥafiẓnā min Tafarūqi Kalimatinā wa-'aṣamnā min Shatāti 'amrinā walā taj'alna firaqan wa-shī'an, nukhālifu b'aḍhanā wa-J'al Ṣalātanā lil-bala'i waqīatan, wa-lil amraḍi shāfīyatan, wa-J'al Tilāwatanā lil-Qur'āni Mūnjīyatan, wa-min an-anāri kāfīyatan wa-J'al Nufusanā Ṣāfīyatan wa fī-l Ākhirati Rāḍhīyatan, yā man lā taḍhī'u 'indahu al-wadayī'u.

Translation:

O Allah, make the Holy Qur'an our strength and support, and the pure Sunnah our love and extension. Protect us from the division of our words, and the scattering of our affairs Do not make us divide and sect from each other. And make our recitation of the Qur'an a deliverer and savior from hellfire. And make our souls pure so that they are not lost.

Source: Ṣaḥiḥ Muslim

Obedience (Du'ā al-Qunut)

اللهمّ إنا نستعينك ونؤمن بك، ونتوكل عليك ونثني عليك الخير ولا نكفرك، اللهم إياك نعبد، ولك نصلي ونسجد، وإليك نسعى ونحفد، نرجو رحمتك ونخشى عذابك، إن عذابك الجدَّ بالكفار مُلحق.

Transliteration:

Allāhumma innā nastaʿīnuka wa nu'minu bika, wa-natawakalu ʿalaīyka wa-nuthnī ʿalaīyka akhaīyra wa lā nakfuruka, Allāhumma Iyyāka n'abudu, wa laka nuṣalī wa-nasjud, wa ilaīyka nas'a wa naḥfidh, na-rju raḥmataka wa-nakhsha' ʿadhābaka, inna ʿadhābaka al-Jidda bil-kufāri mulḥiq.

Translation:

O Allah, we seek Your help and believe in You. We trust in You, we praise You for the good and we are not ungrateful to You.

O Allah, we worship You, we pray to You and we prostrate before You. We seek You, we supplicate to You, we hope for Your mercy, and we fear Your punishment, for Your severe punishment will surely befall the disbelievers.

Source: Al-Albānī

Strengthening of the Faith

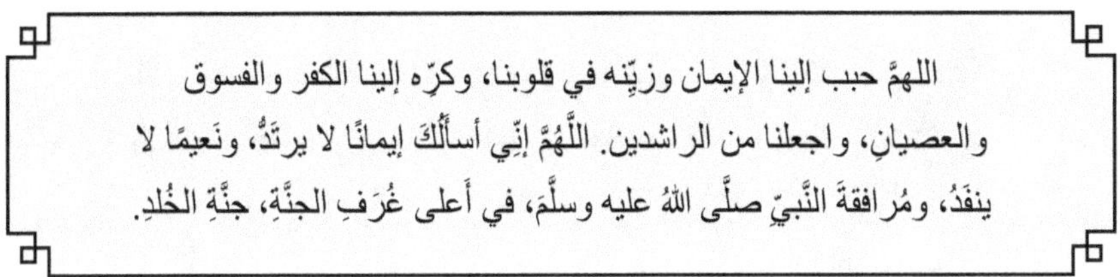

Transliteration:

Allāhumma ḥabbib 'ilaīyna al-'imāna wa-zayīnhu fī Qulubinā, wa-Kerrihi 'ilaīyna al-kufra wal-fusuqa wal-iṣyāni, wa-J'alna min al-rashidāna. Allāhumma innī as'alluka Īmānan lā yartaddu, wa-Na'īyman lā yannfadu, wa-murāfaqata al-Nabī Ṣallal-lahu'alaīhi wasallama, fī 'āla ghurafill Janati, Janati al-Khuldi.

Translation:

O Allah, endear faith to us and make it beautiful in our hearts. And make disbelief, immorality and disobedience hateful to us, and make us among the rightly-guided.

Oh God, I ask you for faith that does not turn back, bliss that does not end, and to accompany the Prophet, may God bless him and grant him peace, in the highest rooms of Paradise, the Garden of Eternity.

Source: Ṣaḥiḥ Al Musnad 833

Consolidation of Faith

اللَّهُمَّ لَكَ الْحَمْدُ كُلُّهُ، اللَّهُمَّ لاَ قَابِضَ لِمَا بَسَطْتَ، وَلاَ مُقَرِّبَ لِمَا بَاعَدْتَ، وَلاَ مُبَاعِدَ لِمَا قَرَّبْتَ، وَلاَ مُعْطِيَ لِمَا مَنَعْتَ، وَلاَ مَانِعَ لِمَا أَعْطَيْتَ. اللَّهُمَّ ابْسُطْ عَلَيْنَا مِنْ بَرَكَاتِكَ وَرَحْمَتِكَ وَفَضْلِكَ وَرِزْقِكَ، اللَّهُمَّ إِنِّي أَسْأَلُكَ النَّعِيمَ الْمُقِيمَ الَّذِي لاَ يَحُولُ وَلاَ يَزُولُ. اللَّهُمَّ إِنِّي أَسْأَلُكَ النَّعِيمَ يَوْمَ الْعَيْلَةِ، وَالأَمْنَ يَوْمَ الْحَرْبِ، اللَّهُمَّ عَائِذًا بِكَ مِنْ سُوءِ مَا أَعْطَيْتَنَا، وَشَرِّ مَا مَنَعْتَ مِنَّا. اللَّهُمَّ حَبِّبْ إِلَيْنَا الإِيمَانَ وَزَيِّنْهُ فِي قُلُوبِنَا، وَكَرِّهْ إِلَيْنَا الْكُفْرَ وَالْفُسُوقَ وَالْعِصْيَانَ، وَاجْعَلْنَا مِنَ الرَّاشِدِينَ. اللَّهُمَّ تَوَفَّنَا مُسْلِمِينَ، وَأَحْيِنَا مُسْلِمِينَ، وَأَلْحِقْنَا بِالصَّالِحِينَ، غَيْرَ خَزَايَا وَلاَ مَفْتُونِينَ. اللَّهُمَّ قَاتِلِ الْكَفَرَةَ الَّذِينَ يَصُدُّونَ عَنْ سَبِيلِكَ، وَيُكَذِّبُونَ رُسُلَكَ، وَاجْعَلْ عَلَيْهِمْ رِجْزَكَ وَعَذَابَكَ. اللَّهُمَّ قَاتِلِ الْكَفَرَةَ الَّذِينَ أُوتُوا الْكِتَابَ، إِلَهَ الْحَقِّ.

Transliteration:

Allāhumma laka al-Ḥamdu kulluhu, Allāhumma lā Qābiḍha limā basaṭṭa, wa lā muqarriba li mā bā'adta, wa lā mubā'ida li mā Qarrabta, wa lā mu'ṭīa li mā man'ata, wa lā mān'a li mā 'Āṭayta. Allāhumma absuṭ 'alaīyna min barakātika wa-raḥmatika wa-faḍlika wa-razqika, Allāhumma innī as'aluka an-na'īm al-muqīm al-ladhī lā yaḥulu wa lā yazūlu. Allāhumma innī as-aluka an-na'īma yauwma al-'aīylati, wa al-Amna yauwma al-Ḥarbi, Allāhumma 'Āīydhan bika min sū'i ma 'Āṭaīytana, wa-Sharri mā man'ata minnā. Allāhumma ḥabbib 'ilaīyna al-'imāna wa-Zaīyinhu fī Qūlubina, wa-karrih ,ilaīyna al-kufra wal-fūsuqa wal-'iṣīyāna, wa-J'alnā mina al-Rāshidīna. Allāhumma tawaffanā Muslimīna, wa-aḥyīnā Muslimīna, wa-alḥiqnā bi aṣ-ṣāliḥīna, ghaīyr khazāya wa lā maftūnīna. Allāhumma Qatil al-kafarata al-ladhīna yaṣuddūna 'an sabīlika, wa-yakadhibūna Rusūlaka, wa-J'al 'alaīyhim Rijzaka wa-'adhābaka. Allāhumma Qātil al-kafarata al-ladhīna ūtū al-kitāba, 'ilah al-Ḥaqqi.

Translation:

O Allah, all praise is due to You. O Allah, none can contract what You expand nor bring near what You put far away. No one can put far away what You bring near. No one can give what You withhold, nor withhold what You give. O Allah, give us some of Your blessings, Your mercy and Your favor and provide for us!

O Allah, I ask You for the constant blessing that is neither changed nor removed. O Allah, I ask You for blessings on the day of extreme poverty and for security on the day of fear. Allah, I seek refuge in You from the evil of what You give us. O Allah, let us love faith and adorn our hearts with it. Let us hate disbelief, deviation, and rebellion. Let us be of the righteous.

O Allah, let us die as Muslims and let us live as Muslims and join us to the righteous, who are neither disappointed nor oppressed.. O Allah, fight the disbelievers who block Your way and who deny Your messengers. Lay disgrace and punishment upon them. O Allah, fight the disbelievers who have been given the Book, O Lord of Truth.

Source: Ṣaḥiḥ Al-Albānī

Thanks to Allah and His Prophets

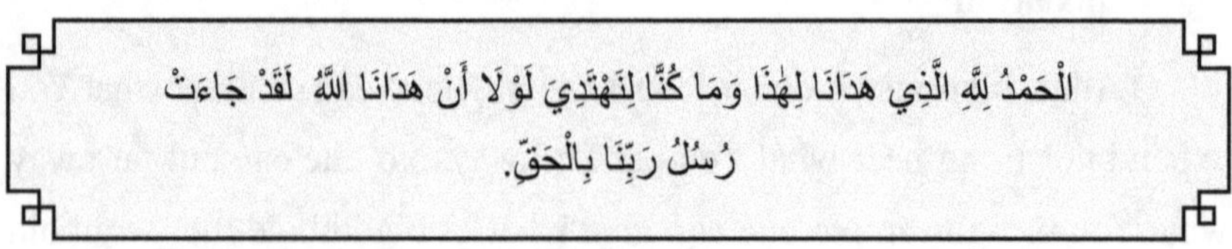

Transliteration:

Alhāmdu-lillāhi al-ladhī hadāna li-hādhā wa mā kunna li-nahtadia laulā an hadānā Allāhu laqad Jā'at Rūsūlu Rabbinā bil-Ḥaqqi.

Translation:

Praise be to Allah for guiding us to this. We would have never been guided if Allah had not guided us. Indeed, the messengers of our Lord have brought the truth.

Source: Surah Al-'Ārāf 7:43

IMPRINT

Salah Moujahed (author)

BAAB Publishing (publisher)

c/o BAAB Ltd
59, Mere Road
B23 7LL Birmingham | United Kingdom
salah@muslimnotebooks.com
Copyright© Salah Moujahed
All rights reserved